Nature with Art

Classroom and Outdoor Art Activities with Natural History

Susie Gwen Criswell

A Spectrum Book

Prentice-Hall, Inc.,
Englewood Cliffs, New Jersey 07632

A SPECTRUM BOOK

Library of Congress Cataloging-in-Publication Data

Criswell, Susie Gwen.
   Nature with Art.

   (Art & design series) (PHalarope books)
   "A Spectrum book."
   Bibliography
   Includes index.
     1. Natural history—Study and teaching. 2. Nature
(Aesthetics) 3. Learning by discovery. I. Title.
II. Series.
QH51.C84 1986   372.3'57   85-31702
ISBN 0-13-610304-9

Printed in the United States of America

10 9 8 7 6 5 4 3 2 1

for John

I would like to thank Mary E. Kennan, my editor at the Prentice Hall Press, for believing in *Nature with Art* and encouraging me to complete the book. This has been a two-year project, the majority of which was written in Foresta, within Yosemite National Park. I have had the privilege of working with the fine staff of the Yosemite Institute during this time, and it is to these people I want to extend grateful recognition. Individuals I wish to thank are Vince Kehoe, Kathleen O'Connell, Elizabeth Hardie, Maggie Rivers, MaryBeth Hennessy, Bar Turner, Bob Pavlick, Lisa Fox, Pete McGee, Larry Prussin, and Pat O'Donnell for their support and assistance. Bobbie Criswell and Pat Perry gave this project invaluable assistance. And finally, a special thanks to my family for their support, and in memory of my grandfather.

For permission to reprint the illustrations on pages 4, 7, 11, 37, 41, 81, 83, 85, 88, 96, 108, 111, 113, 120, 121, 130, and 133, grateful acknowledgment is extended to Shauna Ellett.

For permission to reprint the illustrations on pages 16, 20, 31, 45, 60, and 90, grateful acknowledgment is extended to Erika Perloff.

For permission to reprint the illustrations on pages 13, 46, 107, and 116, grateful acknowledgment is extended to Kathy Darrow.

For permission to reprint the photographs on pages 24, 34, 57, and 64, grateful acknowledgment is extended to Roger McGeehee.

The drawings and photographs on pages 1, 9, 18, 22, 26, 29, 49, 52, 53, 55, 59, 62, 66, 68, 70, 73, 75, 79, 89, 92, 94, 100, 101, 103, 118, 127, 128, 132, and 135 are by the author.

Excerpt from *Everett Ruess: A Vagabond for Beauty* by W. L. Rusho with the letters of Everett Ruess, copyright by Gibbs M. Smith, Inc., 1983, published by Gibbs M. Smith, Inc./Peregrine Smith Books.

Excerpt from *The Natural Way to Draw* by Kimon Nicolaides. Copyright 1941 by Anne Nicolaides. Copyright renewed 1969 by Anne Nicolaides. Reprinted by permission of Houghton Mifflin Company.

Excerpt from *View from the Oak* by Judith and Herbert Kohl. Copyright in 1977 by Herbert Kohl. Reprinted by permission of Sierra Club Books.

Contents

Foreword

Appreciation of our natural world is a subject that continues to receive more and more attention in today's educational circles. In this time of declining resources, teachers and parents are increasingly taking their children outside to discover nature. *Nature with Art* is a book that encourages young people to "see the world" through drawing activities and gain new perspectives that will assist the development of their future thoughts and actions toward our fragile planet.

I have observed Susie Gwen Criswell develop this book from an idea to an important educational tool. The book presents activities based on the philosophy that experiential education offers a balanced approach to learning; the activities are designed so that the children directly experience nature and heighten the use of their senses. The natural history information and art lessons *Nature with Art* offers were assembled and tested while Susie worked as an instructor for the Yosemite Institute. Her fellow staff members are honored to have been part of the process. We see this book as an effective aid for both outdoor and classroom educators. I encourage teachers to experiment with these activities and adapt them to their style of teaching.

Patrick O'Donnell
President, Yosemite Institute

Preface

I walk in the woods with children daily. They come from all over California to feel the spray of Yosemite's waterfalls, lie in the meadows, and climb over the top of granite boulders. My employer, the Yosemite Institute, encourages the students to come closer to the natural world and to learn what it has to teach them. Recently, I asked a group of ten-year-olds to draw any tree they thought was special. The trees that encircled us began to gain greater significance in the eyes of the young artists. The trunks, branches, leaves, and protruding roots drawn by the children became a part of their natural world. The trees became special to each child, largely because she or he took the time to really see them.

The art activities and natural history information in *Nature with Art* are for those of us who spend time outdoors with children. This book will be useful whether you are a parent, teacher, scout leader, or camp counselor. The activities can be molded to meet your children's level of interest. Observe the table of contents, read through the pages of information, and take the ideas and inspiration outdoors with the children.

The fifty-three activities are divided into four natural history categories: Plants, Animals, People and Places, and Earth Science. Natural history information is provided to supplement what you might know about nature. Following each nature question is an art activity that is explained and illustrated. Each lesson connects the natural creative urges of children with the ever-creative cycles of nature.

This discovery process need not happen only in grand places such as Yosemite National Park. A schoolyard, a city park, a local pond—all have wildlife, plants, and weather to observe. The wildlife might be a string of ants marching along cracked pavement or a song sparrow perched on a neighbor's rooftop. The plants may be the neglected weeds on a softball field or the budding tree in a nearby lawn. A growing cumulus cloud or the sun's reflection on water may also lend themselves to discovery through art. The curiosity children have for the outdoor world will grow and develop when an interested adult takes the time to observe these places with them.

I have written *Nature with Art* because there is great merit in focusing children's attention closer to their environment. Young people who learn to appreciate the pattern of a snowflake, the texture of a tree's bark, or the colors of dawn may carry into adulthood a sense of discovery and a bond with nature. This new outlook can, for both the child and the adult, create a growing interest, appreciation, and love for nature that can last a lifetime.

I believe in the power of art. It has been with us since we first scratched animal symbols onto a cave wall or made pots out of the earth's clay. Our art is a primary reflection of the natural world. It is still the universal language that connects all cultures of this planet to one another. If used to study nature, children's artwork can remind them of their connection to one another and the rest of the planet. The activities in this book can help children use art to gain a greater awareness and understanding, and thus a greater appreciation for their natural environment.

Plant
Investigations 1

If facts are the seeds that later produce knowledge and wisdom, then the emotions and the impressions of the senses are the fertile soil in which the seeds must grow. The years of early childhood are the time to prepare the soil.
Rachel Carson
The Sense of Wonder

Plants are at your fingertips. All year-round you can take a walk out in your local park or nearby woods and notice this amazing living force. We often look at plants as solely decorative, enjoying their coolness and colors. This world of chlorophyll may grow so readily that we take it for granted and do not take the time to appreciate how significant it is for the earth and for ourselves.

Plants are the living force which sustain all other life forms on this planet. They are the lowest link in the food chain, therefore the most consumed, and are a vital source of energy. Plants transform the sun's energy into sugars through photosynthesis to feed themselves. Once eaten, they indirectly pass the sun's energy on to the consumer. Plants sustain the soil by decomposing, thereby enriching it, and by holding it in place, not allowing the wind or water to erode it. Through plants, we can appreciate our link to not only the sun, but also to the soil and rain which allow them to grow.

Plants are classified in many forms. The ferns, mosses, algae, fungus, wildflowers, and giant sequoia are all members of the plant kingdom. The different seasons affect this variety of forms in many ways. The deciduous trees close up shop for the winter and drop their leaves, while the conifers do their best to shed snow from their needles to avoid having to grow all new needles the next spring. Many plant seeds lie dormant in the soil during the winter. The seeds of annual plants pop up in the spring, flower in the summer, give off seeds in the fall, and repeat this cycle each year. Roots of perennial plants send forth a plant of the same roots every year, sometimes for decades.

This chapter offers many different ways to acquaint children with the plant world around them. Trees are explored with linear drawing, wood carving, and sawdust modeling dough. The plant habitat is brought closer through drawing from a still-life, hand-lens drawing, and printmaking from nature. Wildflowers and garden plants are illustrated through plant pressing, dyeing from vegetable matter, and corn husk dolls. The more children draw and make crafts with their local plants, the more they will regard them as a part of their natural environment. This chapter's art activities will encourage you and the children to look closer at plants and have them as a more integral part of your world.

BACK-TO-BACK DRAWING

A child holding a leaf in her hand is asked to describe it to her friend who cannot see the leaf. The two children sit with their backs supporting one another, and the challenge is on. The leaf is pressed firmly in the palm, sniffed lightly, held up to the light for closer inspecti'n, and descriptive words are spoken. The "unseeing" friend interprets those words and draws what he hears: words describing shape, line, texture, and the smell of the leaf. This activity promotes close observation of things found in nature. Slowing down and taking time—not only looking at a shell, pine cone, or leaf, but also describing it—keeps the memory of the object with the child longer. Keeping a child in suspense of his partner's object increases curiosity as he draws what he believes to be described. The child who is describing the object is truly "seeing" it by holding and describing that leaf, shell, or pine cone.

Indoor or Outdoor Activity
Time Needed: 30 minutes
Materials Needed: Paper, pencils, "found objects" from nature, drawing boards

Figure 1–2 The children develop their abilities to see and describe nature in back-to-back drawing.

1. Have the children find a partner.

2. One person from each pair should choose an object that he can describe to his partner. He should not allow his partner to see it.

3. The children sit back to back with one person holding the object and the other person preparing to draw.

4. The object should be described without mentioning what it is called. Instead, the child holding the object should mention how big it is, what it reminds her of, what color it is, and what it feels like.

5. While listening to this description, the drawing partner illustrates what he hears.

6. Have the children compare the drawing and object. Switch roles, and repeat this activity.

Why Do Trees Have Leaves?

1. Leaves are the powerhouse of the tree; they allow the tree to grow. Through photosynthesis they turn sunlight into sugar energy, which supplies food to the tree. Most leaves are flat and wide to catch the most sunlight.

2. Deciduous trees have leaves that fall off each autumn and grow back each spring. The leaves are shed because they would either freeze or collect snow and break branches.

3. The veins in a leaf are very important, just as the veins in our bodies are important. Leaf veins carry water through the leaf and also send the sugars down into the rest of the tree.

4. Leaves on trees create shade. Shade provides for as much as 20°F difference of temperature in an area. Tree leaves are a passive energy source, because in the summer they provide shade to cool an area, and in the winter they are shed, exposing the area to the sun's warmth.

5. There are pocket manuals for identifying trees all over the United States. For a catalog of these tree keys, write to: Nature Study Guild Publishers, Box 972, Berkeley, Calif., 94701.

NATURE RUBBINGS

Textures from nature can be studied with nature rubbings and used in art work. Your group of children should search outdoors for textures, such as: the roughness in tree bark, the patterns in lichen, the coarseness of sand, or the symmetry of a leaf. The textured object is placed under the drawing paper and the child firmly presses the crayon while drawing over the paper. This rubbing can be incorporated into another drawing, or combined with several rubbings to create a texture collage, or the textured object may be used repeatedly to create a pattern. The child can also use only part of the texture and then incorporate it in a drawing from the imagination.

Indoor or Outdoor Activity
Time Needed: 30 minutes
Materials Needed: Paper, crayons, textured objects from nature, drawing boards

1. Have the children select objects from nature that have a texture they find interesting.
2. Have them lay it flat on their drawing board with paper over it. Encourage them to place their object under their paper with a sense of design, not necessarily right in the center of their paper.
3. The children should take their crayon and make a steady shading motion over the whole piece of paper, causing the relief of the object below to show through.
4. The textured design can be incorporated into another drawing, the texture can be repeated, or the drawing can be left as is.

What Is Bark Good For?

1. Trees have bark as a protective strategy against insects, fire, and weather. Bark also acts as an insulator against freezing ice and snow.

2. The cracks, or fissures, in bark have pockets of tissue that allow a gas exchange to occur between the air and the interior of the stem. These pockets of tissue are called *lenticels*.

3. Under the hard crusty layer of bark on a tree exists the *phloem*. As the phloem gets older and crushed toward the outside of the tree, it contributes in making the bark. The younger layers of the phloem transport sugars from the leaves to various parts of the tree. This sugar content of the phloem was recognized in North American Indian tribes. Some tribes stripped it from Douglas fir trees and used the dried strips as food for winter and emergencies.

4. Bark has a variety of thicknesses in all trees, especially in conifers. It frequently attains a width of 3 inches or more, and in extreme cases, such as the Giant Sequoia, it may even reach 3 feet in thickness.

5. A dull red dye can be obtained from the younger bark of the Eastern Hemlock, which is also a source of tannins for shoe leather. Native Americans made a poultice for scrapes and cuts by pounding the hemlock's inner bark. Some fibers in barks are used to make ropes.

6. Bark provides a partial diet for mice, squirrels, and deer.

Figure 1–3 Drawings can be made by rubbing a crayon over paper on top of any texture from nature.

7. Bark acts as a habitat or home for many insects, woodpeckers, tree frogs, and spiders.

DRAWING FROM A STILL-LIFE

Drawing from a still-life enables the children to warm up to the idea that everybody can draw. They do the exercise without looking at their paper, thereby allowing them not to judge their work as "good" or "bad," but to simply "draw." Drawing can be an intimidating experience for those expecting to capture the exact image they are seeing. Drawing is not photography. Getting the child's hand to relax with the pencil can be the most difficult task when getting a person comfortable with the idea of drawing.

Indoor or Outdoor Activity
Time Needed: 30 minutes
Materials Needed: Paper, pencil, objects from nature, drawing boards

1. Have each child pick up an object found from nature—such as pine cones, sticks, rocks, or shells–and place them together in an arrangement called a still-life.

2. The children should sit around the still-life and prepare to draw.

3. Explain that they will be asked to draw the arrangement without looking at their paper. They must make every effort to keep their eyes on the still-life and not on their paper while they draw.

4. Letting their pencil move about the paper while their eyes travel around the still-life will keep the group's curiosity high as to what their drawing looks like. If their pencil should run off the page, they should put it back on where it feels right.

5. When they are finished, usually in about five to ten minutes, have the children turn their paper over, without looking at their drawing.

6. A second drawing should be done, this time allowing the children to look from their paper to the still-life. This

drawing usually takes about twice as long and demands a more self-critical concentration.

7. Have them turn over the first drawing and compare the two. Talk about the differences in doing the two drawings. Ask the children in which drawing did they feel they were seeing the still-life better? And which one did they like better?

What Is Duff?

1. Duff is the organic material on the forest floor. Duff includes leaves, branches, needles, animal droppings, decomposed trees, dead animals, water and air.

2. Duff is the top layer of soil. As it decomposes, it mixes with minerals to form new soil.

3. Duff is broken down to form soil by bacteria, fungi, and saprophytes, types of vegetation that do not depend on photosynthesis and chlorophyll to live. They obtain energy instead from decaying organic matter found in the duff or right below it.

Figure 1–4 Pine cones, feathers, and other objects picked up from outside provide materials to draw.

4. The tree makes its own soil by depositing its leaves, branches, and bark onto the forest floor. After dying, the tree joins in the duff layer to be decomposed by bacteria to form soil. This soil then, in turn, provides the necessary germination layer for a new tree to begin its life.

5. Duff acts as an insulator to keep the ground from freezing, protecting the tiny life forms living under this humus layer.

6. "We owe our entire existence to six inches of topsoil and the fact that it rains." Quoted from *The Cocklebur*.

HAND-LENS DRAWING

The hand-lens drawing activity can focus the child's attention on the tiny, microscopic worlds found in nature. While on a walk, have the children carry a hand-lens or a magnifying glass. The tools allow them to observe the miniature life systems found in nature. Mosses, lichens, and leaf structures are common objects that become fascinating when observed in detail. Have the children draw their findings. Pausing, magnifying, and then drawing these objects triggers the children's imaginations to see beyond the surface of things.

Outdoor Activity
Time Needed: 30–45 minutes
Materials Needed: Paper, pencils, hand-lens or magnifying glass, drawing boards

1. Equip each child with a hand-lens or magnifying glass and drawing tools, and take a walk. Walk to where there are mosses, lichens, fungi, grasses, or leaves to be studied.

2. Encourage the children to separate and choose a place for quiet study of the area. Have them get close to the subject matter with their hand-lens.

3. The children should illustrate what they have isolated and magnified. Their drawing should cover the entire page.

Figure 1–5 While looking through magnification, new worlds may open up which the children can illustrate.

4. Let them know they are to work for 15 minutes trying to capture all of the tiny things they see.

What Are Lichens?

1. Lichens are a prime example of the symbiotic relationship. That is, lichen is made from a combination of two other plant forms, fungus and algae.

2. The algae supplies the food for both organisms. The fungus protects the algae from harmful light intensities; it also takes in and stores water and minerals for both organisms. The fungus is a controlled parasite in that it can destroy algae cells.

3. There are 25,000 known species of lichens.

4. Lichens grow very slowly, at a maximum rate of one quarter inch a year. They are capable of living to an age of 4500 years or more. Capable of withstanding terrific hardships, they can be found living on bare rocks in the blazing sun of the desert, in the

bitter cold of the Arctic and Antarctic regions, on trees, or just be-low the snowline on mountains.

5. Lichens can go for a long time without water by going into a dormant state. During these dormant phases the environmental extremes do not bother them.

6. Lichens are very sensitive to pollution, particularly sulphur dioxide. Environmental studies record a lichen's reaction to the air to study pollution amounts in certain areas.

7. Large mammals such as reindeer and caribou can survive on a type of lichen. Lichens are not so tasty for humans, and when consumed, may be irritating to the intestines. Ancient Egyptians ground up lichens for flour, and the Swedes made bread out of reindeer lichen flour.

8. Lichens are evident in many colors: greens, reds, yellows, purples, blacks, oranges, plus others. This rich variety of color is often used to make natural dyes for fabrics.

LINEAR DRAWING

In linear drawing activity the children draw, not what the object from nature looks like, not even what it is, but what it is *doing*. The purpose is to have the young artist feel how the branches of a tree lift or droop, or how a hill rises and falls, and then make a drawing of this growth direction. These drawings are done in a continuous line, with no regard for shading or realistic portrayal. This continu-ous line should be drawn rapidly, from top to bottom, without tak-ing the pencil off the paper. As the eye follows the movement of the shape, the pencil should flow with it. There is no right or wrong linear drawing. This is a good warmup exercise, encourag-ing the children to feel comfortable about drawing and, also, to no-tice the different forms in nature.

Outdoor Activity
Time Needed: 30 minutes
Materials Needed: Paper, pencils, drawing boards

1. Tell the group that this is a loosening-up exercise; there is no "right" or "wrong" linear drawing.

2. A linear drawing is the following of the motion found in nature: the movement of a flowing creek, a fallen tree, or a field of grass in the wind.

3. Have the students seated and prepared to draw. A subject close by is pointed out to them. They are to capture the motion of the object in a quick linear drawing. Each drawing should be timed, ranging from 15 seconds to one minute in length.

4. A continuous line is the method used, never picking the pencil up off the paper.

5. After doing ten drawings, have the children discuss which drawings they like better and why.

What Are the Differences Between Conifers and Deciduous Trees?

1. All conifers have cones. Many, if not most conifers are evergreen—that is, green all year round. Not all conifer cones look like cones: any plant whose female flower produces exposed eggs for fertilization and then develops into a "fruit," usually of wood, while ripening, is a conifer.

Figure 1–6 Deciduous trees lose their leaves in autumn.

2. Within the conifer family are found the world's most massive living things, the Giant Sequoias. The conifers definitely hold the record over the deciduous trees in height. No deciduous trees grow over 180 feet or so. Many conifers grow from 250 to 350 feet tall.

3. The deciduous, or broad-leafed trees, are part of the earth's dominant group of plants: the flower bearers.

4. Deciduous trees evolved as an improvement over the conifers. The main advantage was the sap circulation. The structure of their wood adapted to allow a much freer and stronger flow. This allowed the leaves to be able to evaporate more water, photosynthesize quicker, and get more value out of the summer sun.

5. The deciduous trees' main trick to remedy a cold weather freeze is to drop their leaves. Thus bare, the trees are able to withstand a winter without leaves freezing and causing branches to break off. Without any leaves to carry on photosynthesis, deciduous trees do little to no growing in the winter.

6. Conifers grow much older than deciduous trees. They are one of the oldest plant families. They were growing before the deciduous trees even evolved. Yet, the deciduous trees are on the increase and the conifers are on the way out.

7. Conifers grow quicker and taller than the deciduous because they keep their needles year-round, so they therefore carry on photosynthesis year-round. Photosynthesis is the process of converting the sun's energy into food for the tree.

8. There are about 650 species of conifers. Some of the most familiar are pines, firs, spruces, hemlocks, cedars, larches, and cypresses.

9. Deciduous trees, because of their flowers, are more often pollinated by insects while conifers are pollinated more by the wind.

10. Deciduous trees are called *angiosperms*. Conifers are called *gymnosperms*.

11. Some familiar deciduous trees are the elms, walnuts, beeches, oaks, birches, alders, willows, poplars, cottonwoods, aspens, and fruit trees.

PRINTMAKING FROM NATURE

Children can make simple and beautiful prints of pine needles, leaves, plants, and flowers. Printmaking creates a record of the world of flora around the children's neighborhood. The finished prints can be incorporated into drawings, collages, or kept as art pieces in themselves. In this activity, a plant's shape and texture become more apparent.

Indoor or Outdoor Activity
Time Needed: 30 minutes
Materials Needed: Brayer (ink roller attached to a handle), water-base printing ink, piece of glass or plastic sheet, paper, newsprint, plants, 5-in. by 5-in. squares of cardboard.

1. Explain and demonstrate the entire procedure before the children start.
2. Put glass, plants, brayer, and cardboard on newspaper while working.
3. Squeeze out one to two inches of ink onto the glass and roll the brayer back and forth over the entire surface of the brayer—it should make a sticky, tacky sound when rolling.
4. Place the plant on a piece of paper. Roll the inked brayer over it, coating it with ink.
5. Lay your printing paper down on a firm surface, and lay the inked plant facedown on the paper. Cover it with a piece of clean paper and press firmly. A spoon or fingers may be used to press the paper.
6. Lift up the paper and plant gently and inspect the print. Hang it with clothespins to dry for several minutes.
7. The ink washes off the glass, fingers, and brayer easily with soap and water.

Are All Evergreen Needles Alike?

1. There are many different types of evergreen needles. The needles evolved differently, just as the trees did, depending on the

area where they were growing. Each area has a different degree of sunlight and moisture, which puts different stresses on the tree.

2. The tree's distribution of its needles allows it to make better use of the available sunlight. Cedars and white fir are more shade tolerant than some other trees, their needles making better use of the limited sun that they receive.

3. Pine needles are in bunches, anywhere from bunches of two to five. The bunch forms a cylindrical rod if the needles are held together. Cedar needles are scalelike, and fir needles grow individually straight off the stems and branches of the tree.

4. Within evergreen needles there are tubes lined with special cells that secrete resin. This is a substance which prevents the development of fungi and keeps certain insects from attacking the tree.

Figure 1–7 Evergreen needles have a wide variety of shapes and sizes.

5. Evergreen trees do shed their needles. Unlike deciduous trees, they shed their needles continuously and not just once in autumn. Many evergreen trees are evanescent, or self-pruners. This means that the lower branches on the tree are shed, as well as the needles, as they are not exposed to the sun to carry on photosynthesis and are extra baggage for the tree to keep alive. This process also protects the rest of the tree from fire damage. If the lower branches are shed, the fire traveling along the ground will not affect the crown of the tree.

6. The evergreen needles have different shades of green. In the warmer and lower altitudes the needles are a lighter shade. The bull pine, at lower altitudes, has very light needles. The light greyish-green color reflects the sunlight and keeps the temperature of the needles cooler.

DRAWING MOSS AND LICHEN

Mosses and lichens usually go unnoticed in a forest until someone points them out. But once noticed, they seem to be everywhere. There is a tremendous variety of shape, texture, and color to this hearty vegetation. Mosses and lichens can be used as artists' tools as well as studied for their relationship to the rest of the forest. Dipped in paints, these plants make beautiful designs on paper. This activity is helpful in understanding the structure of mosses and lichens as well as creating unique designs.

Outdoor Activity
Time Needed: 30 minutes
Materials Needed: Available mosses and lichens (use those that have fallen onto the ground, do not rip them off the trees or rocks), and tempera paint, drawing paper, bowls, and drawing boards

1. Once the group finds an area where mosses and lichens are growing, explain to them their relationship to the rest of the forest. Lichens are decomposers; they assist in breaking down rocks and plants into soil.

2. Have the children gather some mosses and collect paints, paper, and bowls to work. Dilute the paint with water and pour it into the bowls for dipping the mosses.

3. Let the children experiment, and allow the different textures to form different patterns.

What Is Moss?

1. Mosses are often known as the soft and cool green covering on damp trees, rocks, and along river banks. But there are many kinds of moss. For example, pygmy mosses appear annually on bare soil after rains and are only 1 to 2 millimeters tall. Pygmy mosses can go through their whole life cycle in a few weeks.

2. Mosses, like fungi, have no flowers at all. They reproduce by spores, not by seeds. These spores are released into the air and travel to germinate by way of wind, water, and insects. There are about 20,000 species of mosses currently known.

3. Mosses retain moisture, slowly releasing it into the soil. This helps to reduce flooding and erosion. Peat moss is very absorbent. When tested, 2.2 pounds of peat moss will take up and hold 55 pounds of water. Moss has antiseptic abilities as well to inhibit bacterial and fungal growth.

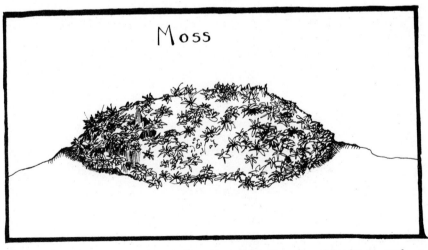

Figure 1–8 Moss is a green non-flowering plant often found in damp, cool habitats.

4. Peat moss is also very important ecologically. Oftentimes in bogs, peat mosses form floating mats over the water and keep conditions so acidic that the growth of bacteria and fungi is inhibited. Without these decomposers present, dead organisms may be preserved in the water for hundreds or thousands of years.

5. The ultra-green, or luminous, mosses—seen around caves and other dark damp places—have an unusual adaptation. The upper surfaces of the cells are curved slightly. This curve serves as a tiny magnifying glass, concentrating the dim light and allowing photosynthesis to occur in an environment that is ordinarily too dark.

6. Birds often use mosses to line their nests, as they are soft and pliable.

PHOTO PAPER DESIGNS

Photo paper is a chemically processed paper that captures the silhouette of any object placed on its surface, after being exposed to the sun for a limited period of time. Children can arrange twigs, leaves, pine needles, or shells on the paper and compose various designs. Photo paper designs focus on shape and structure of objects. They can be incorporated into collages or left out to be displayed individually. The purpose of this activity is to encourage children to develop a sense of balance, arrangement, composition, and discrimination in the objects chosen. This activity is good for training the eye to see arrangements in nature.

Outdoor Activity
Time Needed: 30 minutes
Materials Needed: Photo print paper, objects from nature, container of water large enough to soak paper without folding it, pins. (Note: store paper in a cool, dark place; don't expose the paper until you are ready to print.)

1. Have the children select objects from nature they want to print.
2. If windy, pin papers down on cardboard. Arrange the objects on the photo paper in an appealing design. Expose

it to the sun for 2 to 5 minutes, depending on the cloud cover.

3. Soak the paper in the water for 1 minute, dry the pape flat. The images will sharpen during the drying time.

What Is Photosynthesis?

1. Photosynthesis is the most important process to sustain life on earth. Basically it is an energy-storing phenomenon, taking place in the leaves and other green parts of plants while there is light. The sunlight energy is stored in sugars and starches, which become the food to keep the plant alive.

2. The upper side of the leaf, the side exposed to the sun, begins the process known as *photosynthesis*. The green stuff in leaves is called *chlorophyll*, or the green "blood" of plant life. When the sun hits the chlorophyll it smashes open the water molecules; carbon dioxide and oxygen reconstruct these molecules to form the sugars and starches. These tiny particles of solar energy are called *photons*. Every leaf carries on photosynthesis.

3. Other than creating food for the tree, this process also gives off oxygen that is breathed out through the pores of the

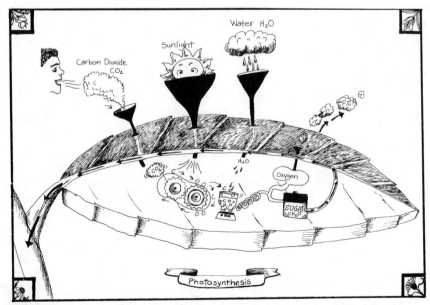

Figure 1–9 Photosynthesis is a process which takes place within all green plants.

leaves. This oxygen exhalation freshens the air with new oxygen. People who have large shade trees or live near the woods actually have an oxygen tent overhead. So photosynthesis furnishes raw material: energy and oxygen.

4. The ultimate size of human populations is very much influenced by plants' ability to take care of the earth's energy needs. Starvation is taking place where there is not enough vegetation.

5. A great deal of photosynthesis takes place in organisms found in the ocean. It is believed that more than 50 percent of the oxygen in our atmosphere originates from the ocean. Knowing this makes it even more evident why we cannot pollute our seas. The pesticide DDT in minute amounts kills the algae that makes our oxygen. If it is sprayed on plants—which get carried down streams and further down by rivers, eventually flowing into the ocean— one can see the potential for destruction of our ocean's important algae.

APPLE DOLLS

Years ago, toys were created from resources that were readily available around the home; pioneers made rag dolls for their children with shrunken apples for heads. Making apple dolls gives modern children an opportunity to create their own toys. Each head takes on its own personality as the aging process of the apple and the children's fingers form the doll's facial features. The body can be made from pipe cleaners, fabric scraps, and string.

Indoor or Outdoor Activity
Time Needed: 2 weeks
Materials Needed: Firm apples, tiny buttons, straight pins, cornsilk for hair, fabric scraps for clothes, pipe cleaners, watercolor paint, knives

1. Have the children peel the apples. The first carving into the apple should be small wedges cut on either side of the nose. Have them cut ¼-in. holes for eye sockets. Make a curved slit for the mouth. Stick the tiny buttons into the eyes with straight pins.

Plant Investigations

21

Figure 1–10 Apple dolls require concentration and safety.

2. Have the children shape the pipe cleaners into the body form and insert it into the head. The head will take a couple of weeks to dry. Have the children reshape the facial features daily as it dries. In about a week, paint the mouth, cheeks, and eyebrows with watercolor paints. Lacquer brushed on the applehead will keep it from decaying further and will give it a glossy appearance.

3. Have the children make clothes from the fabric scraps, and give either cornsilk or yarn for hair, and after two weeks, the apple dolls should look complete.

Where Do Apples Come From?

1. All fruit comes from flowers. The fruit is the mature ovary of the flower. As a mature ovary, the fruit is divided into three parts: the skin, the seed protection, and the fleshy matter.

2. There are about twenty-five species of apples, the most widely cultivated tree fruit crop. The apple tree is native to the temperate zones of both hemispheres.

3. In America, Indians and trappers spread apple seeds, with one fellow Jon Chapman becoming a legendary folk hero known as Johnny Appleseed. He is said to have planted apples abundantly in Ohio and Indiana.

4. Apple trees grow best in climates with distinct winter periods. Yet, apples cannot grow too far north as the growing season would be short.

5. Many apples do not ripen until late fall and may be stored for as long as nine months in temperatures that are just above freezing.

6. In the United States, more than half of the apples picked are eaten as fresh fruit. The others are used for vinegar, juices, jelly, apple butter, pie stock, and applesauce.

7. Apples provide vitamins A and C, are high in carbohydrates, and are an excellent source of cellulose.

WOOD CARVING

Children love to pick up fallen sticks and enjoy the satisfaction of whittling them down. By encouraging the children to look at the fallen pieces of wood as forms they can develop with a knife, the art of woodcarving becomes equally satisfying. By imagining that a fallen branch can become a horse or a dragon, the children begin a creative urge to carve. The forest floor becomes an unlimited source of new shapes for woodcarving.

Outdoor Activity
Time Needed: 1 hour
Materials Needed: Carving knife (pocket knife, Swiss army knife, buck knife) and found pieces of wood. The best woods to carve are: mahogany, walnut, cherry, oak, white pine. Seasoned or dry wood carves better and cracks less.

1. On a walk through a wooded area, look for unusual pieces of wood. Have each child find a piece that has a potential object within.

2. Explain that, for safety, all carving must be done sitting down. Emphasize the need to be careful in handling the knifeblade.

3. Before carving a shape, practice handling the knife by whittling a stick down to a toothpick. Urge the children to work gradually and with control. Make the carving motions down toward the ground.

4. The next carving should be inspired from their imaginations. Carve into the wood, allowing the piece to take on the shape they saw in the wood.

Are There Differences in Types of Wood?

1. Every species of tree offers a different type of wood. This list of mixed conifer and broad-leafed trees mentions several unique features of their wood:

Figure 1–11 The giant sequoia, though huge and awesome, has a very soft wood, as many conifers do.

a. There are thirty-five species of pines in the United States. Pine, generally known as a "soft wood," is used in the construction industry and to make ships, railroad cars, pulpwood, rafters, studs, turpentine, and rosin. Turpentine and rosin are products of a tree that is wounded and the exuding resin collected and distilled by steam. The part that is liquid and evaporates quickly is the turpentine, and the solid is rosin. Rosin is used to make paper and has many other industrial uses.

b. Sugar pine is known as the "king" of all pines, with a huge trunk, beautiful large cones, and a potential height of 200 feet. Ponderosa pines and the Douglas fir are the two most popular woods used for building. Fifty percent of all U.S. forests are composed of Douglas fir trees.

c. The redwood trees are known for their amazing ability to resist decay. They have a chemical within them that destroys wood-consuming fungi. Redwoods known to have fallen 1000 years ago have been found with their heartwood intact. Cedars are known for their aromatic odors.

d. Oaks are broad-leafed trees or deciduous. Their wood is usually hard and heavy and slow to burn. Oak is a very common timber for building.

e. Ashwood is known for its springiness and recreational uses. Baseball bats, snowshoes, paddles, tennis rackets, and toys are commonly made from ash.

f. Black walnut has the honor of being the finest cabinet-making wood in the United States. These trees are growing more scarce and need to be protected.

g. Cottonwood trees grow very fast, usually along rivers and streams found throughout all parts of the United States. Cottonwood lumber is used for making boxes and crates, because the wood nails well without splitting.

CORNHUSK DOLLS

Cornhusk dolls were made by children during pioneer times. Currently they are a popular craft for many who enjoy making toys

Figure 1–12 Five easy steps to illustrate how to make corn husk dolls.

from simple materials. Both boys and girls can construct cornhusk dolls for toys and gifts. These easy-to-make dolls show the children that their toys need not come from the store, but can be homemade from materials found outdoors that do not require money.

Indoor or Outdoor Activity
Time Needed: 1 hour
Materials Needed: Husks from several ears of corn, string, 7-in. pipe cleaners, soaking pan, black felt pen, glue

1. Remove fresh cornhusks from cob, separate the strips, and bleach them in the sun until completely dry.

2. Soak the shucked strips in warm water for 5 to 10 minutes, to make them pliable. Leave them in the water while you are working.

3. To make the head, tear off a ¼-in. wide strip that is the full length of a husk and roll it into a ball. Make this ball

larger by adding several more ¼-in. wide strips. Tie this "head" so it will not unroll with a string.

4. Make another ball for the upper body. Again use strips of cornhusk and roll them up and tie them secure. Make the ball larger for this upper body, about 1-½ inches in diameter.

5. Wind a 1-in. strip of cornhusk around a pipe cleaner to form the arms.

6. Put the arms between the head ball and the upper body ball and drape a strip of husk over the head, long enough to cover the arms and upper body. Secure the husk under the head with a string. Tie another string under the upper body ball, forming the waist.

7. To make an overskirt, tie the husks at the waist, then let the ends fall down over the string.

8. Glue the corn silk on for hair. Add a hat from cornhusks or fabric straps.

9. Draw facial features with a felt-tip marker.

Where Did Corn Come From?

1. The Indians of tropical America were the first to domesticate and grow corn more than 7000 years ago. They crossbred corn plants from various areas trying to improve the crop. The Indians practiced growing hybrids, mixing the early corn with a wild grass relative called *Tripsacum*. This resulted in a cornlike grass called *Teosinte*. Teosinte was crossbred with true corn and a stronger, larger variety of corn resulted.

2. The corn cob of today yields approximately 1000 kernels, compared to the earliest cultivated cobs that yielded under 50 kernels.

3. Corn is originally a Central American species but grows well where there is a hot, dry climate. It has become one of the most important plants grown in the United States. Corn is as vital to our agricultural needs as it was for the Incas, Mayans, and Aztec Indians.

4. Flint corn, soft corn, sweet corn, and popcorn are all popular corns; but "field" corn is the most widely grown. This type

is mostly fed to livestock from which we receive meat, milk, eggs, fats, leather, and many other products.

5. Besides being eaten as sweet corn or popcorn, a small amount of corn is used to make hominy, corn meal, and breakfast foods. Most of the rest is processed into other foods as starches and in alcoholic beverages.

PLANT PRESSING

During the spring and summer months wildflowers bloom all over the hills, covering the countryside with color. This color is the inspiration for paintings and pastel sketches. For a more direct method of capturing the flowers and their color, try pressing the plants. In a large field of flowers, look for specimens that represent the area. Select carefully a few samples to be pressed. Have the children be aware that they are selecting these plants for their beautiful design and color and to learn more about the flower.

Indoor or Outdoor Activity
Time Needed: It takes 3 to 4 weeks to press flowers.
Materials Needed: Several sheets of newspaper, cardboard, heavy books or bricks, ferns, flowers, leaves, cardboard box

1. Select flowers, leaves, and ferns carefully. Do not deplete an area. Have the children keep the plants in moistened plastic bags while collecting.
2. Lay several sheets of newspaper on the bottom of a cardboard box.
3. Place the plants down flat—not overlapping one another—on the newspaper. Lay several sheets of newsprint on top of the flowers, followed by the cardboard, and finally the heavy books or bricks.
4. Do not disturb the box for 3 to 4 weeks. The flowers and ferns will be pressed with the majority of color intact. Carefully remove the pressed foliage to use in craft projects, to mail to a special friend, or to keep a record of the plants of the children's local area.

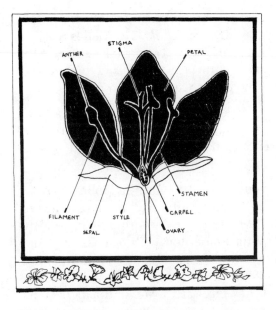

Figure 1–13 The flower's anatomy may be illustrated through plant pressing.

What Are Flowering Plants?

1. More than half of all living plants are angiosperms, or flowering plants. *Angiosperm* means a plant with enclosed seeds. They are a very diversified and widespread form of plant life, and the reason for their success is the flowering part of the plant.

2. Flowers are an efficient reproducer compared to the male and female cones of the conifers. The conifers depend on the wind for pollination, while flowering plants are pollinated not only by the wind, but also by insects and by themselves.

3. Flowers are composed of a thousand variations in color, design, and number of petals, but many have the two sexual organs as a part of their structure. The female part is called the *carpel*, the male part is the *stamen*.

4. The female carpel has a seed-containing ovary at its base and pollen-catching *stigmas* topping the slender supporting *style*. The carpel receives the pollen and holds the seeds, enabling them to be fertilized and to mature.

5. The male stamen is made up of two parts: the thin *filament*, and the pollen-producing *anther*.

6. Both the carpel and stamens are encircled by the petals, which are, in turn, surrounded by the *sepals*. The petals are colored and have adapted to excrete colors and nectar to attract the pollinating insects. The sepals are the original parts of the bud that protected the young flower before it was ready to open.

7. All angiosperms also have roots, stems, and leaves as well as the flowering parts. These structural components provide necessary moisture and nutrients to the plant to allow photosynthesis.

8. Flowers that rely entirely on the wind for pollination are usually small and less showy in color as they do not have to attract insects. Since they do not have colors and perfume to attract the insects for pollination, they have adapted with a mass of pollen much greater than other flowering plants. This vast amount of pollen usually gets released in the early spring before foliage leaves block their way. People with hay fever are aware of this pollen distribution each spring as the wind transports it, triggering their allergies.

DYEING FROM VEGETABLE MATTER

Children can learn to make and use vegetable dyes for dyeing natural fibers such as wool and cotton. Before any fabric can be dyed it must be treated with a dye adhesive, called a mordant, so that it holds the applied dye. Rubber gloves should be worn by anyone mixing and using the mordants and vegetable dyes to protect the skin. The place where the children work should be well ventilated, and they should avoid inhaling the fumes of these relatively nontoxic dyes.

Indoor or Outdoor Activity
Time Needed: 2 days for mordant and dyeing process
Materials Needed: Large enamel kettles (large enough to completely immerse the fabric without spilling), mordant (wool = 1 ounce alum plus ¼-ounce tartar for each gallon of water; cotton = 1 ounce alum plus ¼-ounce baking soda per gallon of water), variety of vegetable dyes, long-handled spoon, clear running water, and clothes line

Figure 1–14 Vegetables from the garden or kitchen make beautiful dyes.

1. Put washed fabric in kettle with required amount of water and mordant necessary (see above), and bring to a boil for one hour, stirring occasionally with a wooden spoon to assure even saturation. Squeeze out excess moisture without wringing the fabric, and hang on the clothes line overnight.

2. To make the dye, gather the desired plants, nuts, and berries while they are young (roots in the fall, leaves as soon as they are full grown, berries when they are ripe). Boil them individually until the described color is reached in the water. Strain out the vegetable matter. Mix and dilute these dyes to obtain a variety of shades of color. Keep the desired colors separate.

3. Add the water, which has been colored by the vegetables, to a kettle of gently boiling water. Immerse the fabric, making sure it doesn't overflow the kettle. Stir the fabric in the kettle until it is the desired color. Remove the fabric and rinse it out in clear running water, squeeze out the excess moisture, and hang it on the clothes line. Make sure that while the fabric is on the line it does not come into contact with the other wet natural fibers.

What Makes a Plant a Vegetable?

1. A *vegetable* is a plant cultivated for its edible parts, whether that be its roots, stems, leaves, or flowers. A *fruit* is the ripened ovary of a flower. Generally, people think of fruits as being sweet and a dessert food, while vegetables tend to be more a salad or main-course dish.

2. The development of agriculture has been the key for the survival of the earth's large population. Native Indians require a hunting-gathering area of over 10 square miles per human. If one figures the inhabitable earth surface as being 30 million square miles, the natural food capacity would never be able to feed the 4.5

Vegetable Dyes

Vegetable Matter	Color
Goldenrod (chop the whole plant into small pieces)	Yellow
Pear or peach leaves	Pale Yellow
Black walnut husks and shells	Yellow-Brown
Sumac leaves (ground to a powder)	Yellow-Brown
Sumac roots	Yellow
Sumac berries	Purple
Sunflower seeds	Blue
Larkspur flowers	Blue
Beets	Red-Violet
Dandelion roots	Dark Pink
Staghorn lichen	Bright Yellow-Green

billion people living on this planet. If people were to return strictly to the hunting and gathering methods of food survival, only one out of 1000 would be able to survive.

3. The wild cabbage is given credit for many modern vegetable staples: from it has developed the green and red cabbages, cauliflower, broccoli, brussels sprouts, rutabaga, and turnip. Many vegetables have been recent additions to our choice of foods, but green cabbages were eaten during the Bronze Age and were popular among the Egyptians and Romans. They also ate watercress, horseradish, and radishes.

4. Red cabbage was not known until the Middle Ages; broccoli and cauliflower were not known until the sixteenth century.

5. Spices are not thought of as vegetables, yet they, too, come from plant matter found all over the earth. Cinnamon originates from the inner bark of an Asian evergreen tree, cloves are the unopened flower buds of a tree, and ginger is the root of a tropical Asian plant.

SAWDUST MODELING DOUGH

Sawdust can be collected from a local construction area, a wood lot, or a nearby forest that has wood taken from it. Sawdust, with its variation in color, texture, and smell, helps us to see the compositions of a variety of trees. The following activity uses sawdust as a main ingredient.

Indoor or Outdoor Activity
Time Needed: 30 minutes plus collecting time
Materials Needed: 1 cup sawdust, ½-cup of common paste or flour paste, cold water, plastic bag and closure, bowl

1. Have the children mix the ingredients in a bowl until it becomes a uniformly pliable dough.
2. Use different colors of sawdust or food dye to make different colors of modeling dough. Keep the dough in the plastic bag in a refrigerator when not using it. Periodic moistening with water will keep the dough fresh longer.

Plant
Investigations

33

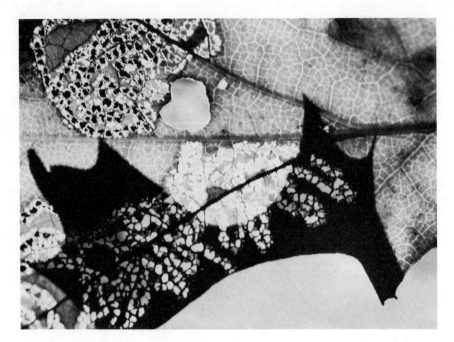

Figure 1–15 The patterns left on autumn leaves illustrate the summer eating habits of insects.

3. Have the children use the dough to mold shapes of objects they observe around them. If left unbagged the shapes will solidify and can be painted, to make toys and gifts.

How Do Insects Use Trees?

1. Many insects have very specialized relationships with trees. Each species of caterpillar requires eating a specific type of leaf in a special season, or it will starve. Oak trees are a favorite food for many species of leaf miners from several orders of insects. Beetles, butterflies, moths, flies, bees, ants, and wasps may burrow between the skinlike layers of the leaves and create a netlike pattern where the tissue is removed. The majority of these netlike tunnels are formed during summer, allowing a multitude of patterned leaves to be found in the fall.

2. The insect world is vast. They occur in almost every habitat, regardless of temperature or altitude, leaving only the ocean

uninvaded. Many people feel that all insects are pests and should be eradicated. But after studying entomology (the science of insects), one can understand that although they may cause damage at times to crops and other vegetation, insects also pollinate flowering plants, decompose plant and animal materials, control other insects, are food for fish, amphibians, birds, and mammals, and are a key to a diversity of wildlife.

3. Often *galls*, or an abnormal growth in a plant caused by other organisms, are due to wasps that lay eggs on the twig. As the larvae hatch and begin to feed, an enzyme is released through the young insect's saliva. This enzyme changes starch in the plant cell to sugar at an excess rate, causing the cells to multiply forming a gall.

4. All the flowering trees, including oaks, dogwoods, fruit trees, plus many others, provide food for insects in their pollen.

5. Aphids are the sucking insects, sap thieves. Their mouths have needlelike tubes with which they suck out the sugary products of photosynthesis. If not for the predacious lacewings and ladybird beetles, the aphids would paralyze foliage.

6. When a tree falls to the forest floor, there are countless decomposers in the insect world ready to break down the remains of the tree into soil. Termites and beetles are the two decomposers that leave sawdust behind them in their eating of dead trees. Other insects of the woodland floor are the silverfish and wood lice, which live in rotting logs.

Animal
Explorations 2

It enriches our understanding of ourselves to move away from familiar worlds and attempt to understand the experience of other animals with whom we share common ancestors. The respect for other forms of life we can gain from these efforts might in some small way help us work toward preserving the world we share.

Judith and Herbert Kohl
The View from the Oak

ANIMAL EXPLORATIONS

Wild animals are fascinating attention grabbers. Bears, bobcats, and fox are subjects children love to see and have stories told about. These mammals are impressive and educational, yet rarely seen. I lived in Yosemite National Park for several months before I saw my first bear, and years before I saw a bobcat, and I have seen only one gray fox. Traces of these hard to see creatures can be detected. Children can be taught to notice tracks in the snow or along a muddy shore, scat, or feces, can be examined, and evidence of browsing or grazing reveals where the animals have been eating. Most children have a natural curiosity about wild creatures and enjoy learning the clues that will help them discover the animals' habitats.

Most wild animals are overlooked. Insects inhabit a hidden world, often found beneath rocks and within rotting logs. Many children think that all bugs are bad. They do not realize that a variety of insects are important for decomposition, pollination, and the food chain. Birds, too, are wild animals. Most of the birds children see in their backyard will never be touched by a human hand. Many birds forage for food, reproduce, and go through their life cycle entirely as wild animals. Along a slow moving stream, fish may be seen swimming in pools or gently against the current, allowing food to float into their gaping mouths. On walks through fields, look for mole tunnels as they criss-cross your trail, listen for crickets chirping in the night, and search for salamanders under damp logs. Wild animals can in fact be found in your own backyard; all you have to do is to take the time to look for them.

This chapter's activities are designed to promote awareness of wild animals and their characteristics. By drawing with a feather and noticing its light weight and smoothness, a child may learn more about birds and flight. Microscope drawing will illustrate to the children that a drop of pond water may be swarming with animals, each one tiny and complete. The spider's intricate weaving of threads may be better understood as the children weave their own threads on a card loom. During these activities the children will look closer at the wildlife which lives around them. The lessons they receive from the activities will be introduced by you, the leader, but taught by the animals which they observe.

DRAWING FROM MEMORY

This activity teaches the children to use their memories recounted from their surroundings as starting blocks for other drawings. While out on an outing, encourage the children to notice a specific subject and ask them to study it. Have the group discuss the subject matter. Have them say what the tree reminds them of, how tall it is, what color it is, what it smells like, what its texture feels like; gather together many recollections as a group. Continue on the walk to another spot and ask the children to now draw the previous subject studied. Mention that they have the liberty to use their imaginations—to put more branches on a tree than they remember the subject had, to put ground cover in that they perhaps do not remember noticing—in short, use artistic license. They should realize that they are using the initial subject as a starting point and allowing their memories' interpretation to complete the drawing. The following activity is another memory-drawing exercise.

Outdoor or Indoor Activity
Time Needed: 30 minutes
Materials Needed: Paper, pencils, objects from nature, drawing boards

1. Have the children gather objects that they can hold in their hands.

2. Encourage the group to compose a still-life in the center of their circle with the objects found.

3. Allow the children to study the still-life for 1 minute silently, without drawing.

4. Have them turn around after 1 minute and, facing away from the still-life, try to draw it from memory (about 2 minutes).

5. Allow them to silently study the still-life for another 1 minute period. The group will be very attentive, more clearly "seeing" the still-life at this second viewing.

6. Have them turn away from the still-life and resume their drawing for 2 minutes.

Figure 2–2 Children's awareness of what is around them is developed when they do memory drawings.

7. The third time they draw, the children can have their drawing in front of them while facing the still-life. Discourage erasures; have them work with "mistakes" rather than starting over. They should draw lines over lines, shapes over shapes if necessary; this will add interest to the drawing.

Do Animals Have a Memory?

1. Animals do use their memories. It used to be generally believed that humans used intelligence and animals used instinct for survival. Now, it is realized that animals do *learn* much of their behavior as well as being born with a genetic ability to perform certain acts.

2. Just as with small children, many animals, from a tiny chick to young turtles, rely on environmental reinforcements to learn to survive. Sensitivity to hot and cold teaches them where to sleep to stay alive, available food sources teach the young where

they can eat to survive, and parental coaching trains young wildlife how to survive predator attacks and where to go for an assured food supply.

3. All animals travel. A journey might be thousands of miles for migration, or inches for eating purposes. Some of their travels involve instinct, but much of the knowledge of "where to go" and "how far" relies on a variety of sensory apparatuses.

4. It is believed that some animals use sonar (echo sounds to establish location), some an incredible sense of smell, some an acute visual ability. Some animals have tiny hairs to detect movement in their surroundings, and some have magnetic detection systems. These methods, plus many more somewhat mysterious sensory devices, allow wildlife to venture forth and learn more about their environment.

PATTERNS FROM NATURE

The shapes found in nature become important tools for understanding how to draw all other forms, for they will always be in some relationship to another object from nature. As John Muir said, "When we try to pick out one thing by itself, we find it hitched to everything else in the universe." Within these shapes we find many different symmetrical patterns and reoccurring shapes. Nature's symmetry found in a butterfly's wings, maple leaves, and insect's body, or a white fir branch all provide a good basis for ideas in design. These patterns can be recorded in the children's sketchbooks and taken home to be incorporated into later drawings.

Outdoor Activity
Time Needed: 1 hour
Materials Needed: Drawing paper, pencils, drawing boards

1. Before going on an outdoor walk, discuss with the children the patterns found in nature. Define *symmetry* as shapes or position of parts that are the same, yet on opposite sides of a dividing line. Put it in terms so that the children will be able to visualize. Mention things to be

found that offer examples of symmetry, such as: leaves, insect wings, or many animal bodies. Other designs in nature do not have symmetry yet suggest a sense of balance, often formed quite chaotically—for example, the design of fallen boulders balanced against one another, or the patterns made by tree trunks. One should also draw the children's attention to the patterns found in ice crystals, sea shells, snow flakes, flowers, and tree rings.

2. Have the children prepared to draw while out on their walk.

3. Have the children record the different patterns in nature they find. Encourage them to notice pine needles, a frog's eggs, or the symmetry of a feather.

4. Have them label each illustration, where it was found and the date. Keep a tally of how many different patterns in nature they can find.

What Is Camouflage Good For?

1. Camouflage often protects the animal by coloring it to conceal the animal within its environment.

2. Some animals' camouflage doesn't always conceal, but instead it gives off false information. For example a very delicious butterfly, the Viceroy, is colored the same as, or mimics, the Monarch butterfly, which is very unpalatable to birds. Birds, therefore, often won't eat the Viceroy because they mistake it for the bad-tasting Monarch.

3. Color concealment is found at all levels of the animal kingdom. The most simple examples of background matching are the fish eggs that exist in the open sea: these eggs, usually transparent, are all but invisible to the eye.

4. In some species, it is the camouflaged nest of the animal that must act to protect the eggs. The nests of birds are often hidden within the branches of the tree, as far from predators as possible.

5. Some animals are known for their ability to change color to camouflage only in a stressful situation. Some fish are noted for

their ability to change colors to blend in temporarily with their background.

6. Some animals actually digest or put on the colors of their host, which makes their appearance blend in with their surroundings to avoid capture. A slow-moving sealike slug, the *nudibranch*, actually ingests portions of its home, living coral. The brilliant colors of the coral show through the *nudibranch*, allowing it to match perfectly with its host, affording good protection from other predators.

7. Some camouflage is related to seasonal changes. Many small mammals adapt a lighter fur coloration during the winter snows. Some animals who do this are hares, weasels, and ptarmigans.

8. Many insects are protected by resemblance to parts of the environment in which they live. Many caterpillars take on the appearance of a twig in coloration and form. Some walking sticks look like dead or green twigs, and others like leaves.

9. Some animals have recognition marks, or signals, to assist in warning others of the species of danger. The white, outer tail feathers of many birds, the white rump on antelope and deer, and the tail on a cottontail rabbit are all warning signals when these species are frightened.

MICROSCOPE DRAWING

Out in the field, gather tiny objects and collect them in match boxes, frisbees, or small fish nets. Example objects are pond larva, frog eggs, whiskers from a cat, or a scraping of some fungus. After returning, examine these objects through a microscope and have the children illustrate what they see. Write down the magnification power next to the illustrations. By enlarging these drawings and coloring in the designs, these illustrations may become future ideas for abstract patterns.

Indoor Activity
Time Needed: 30 minutes to 1 hour
Materials Needed: Microscope, viewing slides, material from nature, paper, pencils, colors, drawing boards

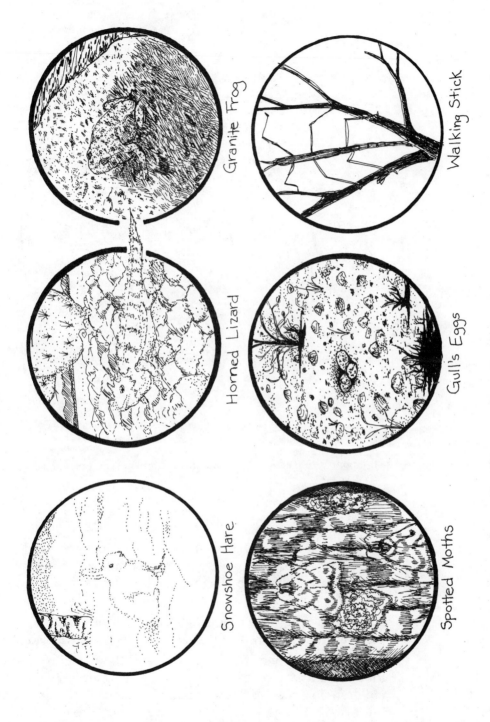

Figure 2-3 Fish, birds, insects, mammals, reptiles, and amphibians have degrees of camouflage in order to survive, reproduce, and keep their species alive.

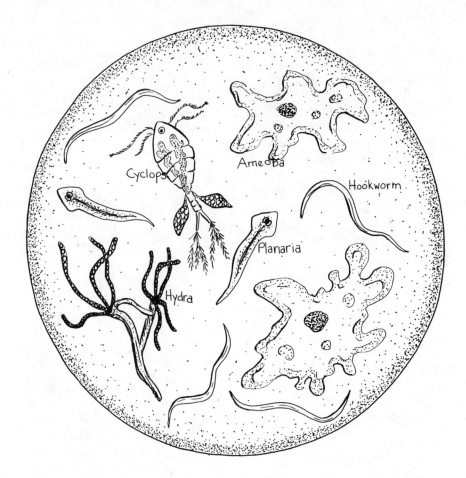

Figure 2–4 A pond study can be illustrated through microscope drawings.

1. On a walk, gather objects from outside to be viewed through the microscope. Excellent examples of objects children may find are decomposing vegetation, insect larva, or pond water.

2. Set the examples up on viewing slides or dishes and have the children prepare to illustrate what is being viewed.

3. Draw the specimens in small form, and then label what they are and the magnified power used. Then have the children do a second drawing using the same specimens, but draw them as large as the entire sheet of paper.

4. Have the children color in the shapes drawn. This second drawing is to be inspired from the microscopic object, yet it should freely use the children's sense of creativity.

What Relationships Do Tiny Animals Have with Big Animals?

1. Most of the animals in the world are *invertebrates*: they have no backbone. Animals with backbones, *vertebrates*, are the most familiar to humans—such as fish, frogs, salamanders, lizards, snakes, turtles, all birds, all mammals—yet vertebrates only comprise 5 percent of the animal kingdom.

2. Many of the invertebrates are very tiny animals. Examples of invertebrates would be jellyfish, corals, flatworms, snails, octopuses, crabs, lobsters, spiders, and all the insects. The group called *protozoa* are one-celled animals that can be found in fresh and salt water, damp soil, and dry sand.

3. Protozoa supply a valuable food source for all kinds of animals. They also can be parasitic to all kinds of animals, including humans. An example is the *sporozoa*, which is a malaria parasite: if taken in by a mosquito and allowed to develop, that mosquito can transmit malaria to humans.

4. Sponges were commonly used by the ancient Romans and Greeks for cleaning their floors and walls, similar to our uses of today. A living sponge looks more like a slimy piece of raw liver than the familiar sponge we see in the house. For a long time people thought sponges were in the plant instead of the animal family, as they do not move around.

5. Insects, also invertebrates, are important in maintaining the balance of nature on land and in lakes and streams (there are virtually no insects in the sea). There are around 80 million known species of insects. The majority feed upon plants: some prefer the nectar and pollen of flowers, others drink the sap, others feed inside leaves, stems, fruits, roots, or seeds. Many insects are of utmost value to humans: bees, flies, butterflies, and other pollinators go from flower to flower collecting pollen for their own use but also carry pollen from one blossom to another, fertilizing plants for future fruits and growth.

6. Plant-eating insects are the food for many carnivores—other insects, spiders, centipedes, frogs, fish, turtles, snakes, birds, mammals, even people. Although most Western people do not consider eating insects, they are nourishing and flavorful food, an important source of fat, and could contribute to protein in the human diet.

7. Insect scavengers enrich the soil by helping to decompose the carcasses of dead animals of all sizes.

TOOLS FROM NATURE

Neither graphite pencils, felt-tip markers, nor ball point pens have existed for a very long time, but drawing has lasted for thousands of years. The first drawings of the early humans were done on bones, on cave walls, and in sandstone. The tools these early people used were pointed sticks, charcoal from the hearth, and natural chalks. Not until the fifteenth century, when paper became abundant, did drawing flourish in the West. These people of the fifteenth century drew with the quill pen, formed from different bird feathers. It was not until the eighteenth century that the pencil, which is graphite mixed with clay encased in wood, was first developed. This gave the artist a tool that did not run out of ink repeatedly, nor did it crumble under the artist's hand. For several centuries artists thought of pencil drawings as merely preparation for more artistic endeavors such as portraits, paintings, clay modelings, or woodwork. Now, drawings are being thought of as works of art in themselves. A good activity for children is to have them experiment making art with tools from nature. This experimentation helps them become aware of how drawing tools originally evolved from natural "tools."

Indoor or Outdoor Activity
Time Needed: 30 minutes to 1 hour
Materials Needed: Feathers, sticks, wild berries, beets, paper, drawing boards. (Instead of berries and beets, you can use tempera paints and bottled inks.)

1. Boil and then simmer the beets and berries. Remove the juice and let it cool, to be used for drawing inks.

2. Collect the feathers and sticks, and sharpen their ends with knives.

3. With the sticks and feathers draw on the paper the bird or tree the drawing tool came from. Also draw the berry bush or vegetable from which the inks came from.

4. These drawing tools will become physical connectors for the children between the arts and nature.

What Good Are Feathers?

1. All birds—and only birds—have feathers. Birds are able to fly largely because of their feathers, their powerful wings, and hollow bones, their warm blood, and respiratory system, and their large, strong heart. Basically these qualities coupled high power with low weight, allowing the bird to fly.

Figure 2–5 The function of feathers is flight, warmth, and camouflage.

2. There are five types of feathers: vaned or contour, down, semiplume, filoplume, and powder down. Though they have different purposes, most feathers are basically the same in construction.

3. Feathers have no living cells, they receive nothing from the body but physical support.

4. The two main jobs of feathers are heat conservation and flight.

5. Oily feathers give buoyancy to water fowl by increasing their volume while only slightly increasing their weight.

6. Feathers serve not only as functions of flight and warmth, but also as color markings. The feathers may serve to camouflage the bird, for reproductive strategies, or they may be recognition marks. Many small perching birds blend in with their surroundings to avoid contact with their predators. Brilliant-colored throat patches or many males' striking colors will attract the female to promote a sexual interaction. Recognition marks, such as the white flash on a junko's feathers, only seen when in flight, warn other junkos that danger may be near. Feathers offering camouflage or recognition marks help keep their species alive.

7. Birds carry more feathers in the winter than in the summer to keep warm.

8. Usually after the breeding season, the worn-out feathers of birds are lost, or molted; within a gradual period, of several weeks to months, they grow back.

PERSONALITY SHIELD

A "personality shield" reflects children's feelings on home, family, and future hopes. On a piece of paper draw the shape of a shield and divide it into four sections. In each of these sections the children are to illustrate a symbol in response to different questions. Some example questions are: What does a symbol of home look like? What does the symbol look like for the person who has the most influence in your life? What is the symbol for your future? Through this activity different aspects of their lives are illustrated.

Indoor or Outdoor Activity
Time Needed: 30 minutes
Materials Needed: Drawing paper, drawing tools, drawing boards

1. With a group seated in a circle, explain how to make personality shields.

2. Distribute drawing materials. The children should then draw any shape they feel illustrates a shield, using the entire sheet of paper.

3. Have them divide their shield into at least four sections.

4. Ask them questions to be answered by illustrations in their shield. Example questions are: What symbol could represent yourself? What is a symbol for your favorite animal? What is a symbol for your favorite season? The children may suggest their own questions, to be illustrated on the shield, if you feel they can volunteer good questions.

What Is the Personality of a Predator?

1. Predators are animals that eat other animals. Predators serve special functions. There are times when predators keep the prey species from becoming overpopulated. When grass eaters—such as deer, mice, and rabbits—become too abundant, predators move in and put them under heavy hunting pressure. When there are fewer prey species available after a heavy hunting time, gradually there become fewer predators because of ators, the prey resume their numbers and the cycle continues.

2. Most predators—such as skunks, bears, cougars—avoid contact with humans and are seen less frequently than many other animals. Most hunt at night.

3. Bears are mostly loners; only during mating time do bears spend time with one another. Females are very protective of their cubs. These cubs are usually born in pairs, but can vary. Bears not only eat other animals but also berries, grasses, and insects. Bears are not true hibernators but simply enter a deep sleep.

4. Raccoons hunt at night, usually along streams or shorelines. Their diet includes frogs, water insects, fish, grasshop-

Figure 2–6 The personality shield encourages the children to explore their own personalities.

pers, and eggs of ground-dwelling birds. Raccoons, who seem to have short tempers, are often heard to be having quarrels and can get into vicious fights. Raccoons make a birdlike churring as a means of communication. They also growl when they are angry.

5. The weasel, an excellent hunter with few equals, is known for its courage in a fight, its intelligence and grace. Weasels hunt by smell rather than sight. Diet includes mice, woodrats, squirrels, chipmunks, birds, and some insects. If the weasel's hunting is good, it will eat half its own weight in 24 hours.

6. Other predators are respectful of the striped skunk, because of the very distinctive odor it can give off. It is always ready to defend itself, but it only discharges its powerful smell when there's a good reason. The skunk is an easygoing animal; it moves slowly, as though it knows its musk glands will ensure safety.

EMOTION DRAWING

Nature creates emotional responses in people. By having children illustrate their emotions and become aware of their source, they may learn to understand themselves and their connection to nature better. The first day of sunshine after two weeks of rain, the first thunderstorm of a summer, or the sounds of a rushing creek are just a few of the examples that create those special moods within children and adults. By learning to make a drawing to express these feelings, the children learn to interpret these moods and to illustrate them through different lines, colors, and shapes.

Outdoor Activity
Time Needed: 30 minutes
Materials Needed: Large variety of colors, paper, and drawing boards

1. While on a nature hike—perhaps during a sunset, while a storm is threatening, or along a quiet creek—have the children spread out and sit quietly alone for 15 minutes. During this "alone time" have them record five different emotions or adjectives to describe the time spent alone.

2. When the children gather together, hand out the paper and the colors. Explain that they are going to draw those five words all on one piece of paper.

Figure 2–7 Sitting on a river's shore, away from the other children, this girl can capture the mood she feels.

3. The children will illustrate their emotions by doing three steps for each emotion; the entire action should take just a few seconds. First, they should say the word aloud. Second, they should choose a color that seems to fit the word. Finally, they should make an abstract mark on the paper to signify the word. Encourage the children not to debate or think too long about their mark, but to move quickly and let themselves be surprised with the outcome.

4. This activity allows the children to understand that abstract images can be inspired from elements of nature and inner feelings.

Do Any Animals in Nature Experience Emotions?

1. It is impossible to know whether wildlife experience the same emotions as humans, that is, grief, happiness, jealousy, anger, fear. Scientists in the lab and out in the field are studying animal life to record their behavior to external stimuli.

2. It has been found that animals do learn much of their behavior and do not rely totally on instinct. By learning different methods of securing food, shelter, and water, wildlife survive to reproduce their species. When animals are observed in the wild, it is evident that they do experience some degree of emotion.

3. One only has to see a mouse scurry away or a deer make a quick retreat into the forest to see that wildlife experience a degree of fear or of self-preservation.

4. We can see the emotion of anger in a chattering squirrel whose habitat has been invaded, or in a mother goshawk swooping down to protect her nest.

5. During mating periods, the bellowing of elephant seals can be heard for quite a distance. The sound arises from the males fighting over the females, displaying what appears to be jealousy and aggressive domineering behavior.

6. After feasting on a night of mice, pocket gophers, woodrats, and rabbits, we might see a coyote lazily looking for a hidden place to lie down and sleep for part of the day. A sense of sleepy contentment can be detected in this usually hyperactive coyote.

7. Watching mother animals in the wild, one definitely observes the emotion of affection they show for their young. Even the mother bat shows much affection for her baby and bathes it daily with her tongue.

PAPER MASH MASKS

Many inspirational faces appear in nature: the mountain lion, the catfish, the barnyard pig, or a great blue heron. Most of the faces in nature in general utilize the same features as humans—that is, eyes, ears, nose, teeth—yet each animal face is different in "personality." A child's imagination and interpretation can capture these faces by creating paper-mash masks. A balloon, newsprint, glue, and water are the main tools needed. Yarn, paint, varnish, and fabric scraps provide added detail and color. Children can wear their masks when playing, acting, or for parties. Try to interpret the faces of the animals in your local area, from ants to sparrows to coyotes.

Figure 2–8 Mask making provides a creative way to study animal faces.

Indoor Activity
Time Needed: Three different 1-hour periods
Materials Needed: Large round balloons, newspaper, glue, water, tempera paint, yarn, varnish, scissors

1. Before each 1-hour period, have a mask completed as far as they should get that day, to demonstrate.

2. The water-glue mixture is one part glue to three parts water. Have it mixed in one bowl for every three children.

3. Have the children tear many strips of newsprint (l-in. by 4-in.) and soak them in the glue mixture. Have them blow up their balloons; each balloon should be large enough to cover the child's face.

4. Work with one strip at a time. Remove the excess water from the strip by running your fingers down the strip. Lay each piece of strained newsprint over the balloon surface. Laying them in random directions of several layers will make the balloon stronger. Allow the balloons to dry; it will take several days. Store them carefully. Have the children put their names on their balloons.

5. The second session will be to build the features on the mask. Remake the glue mixture as before, but cut the newsprint in smaller pieces and soak it longer.

6. With this mash mixture of newsprint build features such as ears, snouts, and cheeks. Lay longer strips (l-in. by 4-in.) over the mash to hold the features in place. Again allow several days to dry.

7. In the third session the children may paint, add yarn, and varnish their masks. Tempera paint dries pretty quickly, and then the yarn can be glued down; the varnish is the final coat over the paint. The back of the mask should be cut away, the balloon should be removed, eye holes should be cut, and a string is attached to tie them on the back of the children's heads.

Why Do Animals Have Whiskers?

1. Most animals who have whiskers use them as sensory detectors. The whiskers help them figure out where they are. On

Figure 2–9 The whiskers of the marmot help it to explore its rocky habitat.

most mammals their whiskers are as wide as the widest part of their body. This enables the animal to stick its head in a hole and figure out if its whole body can get through that hole. If its whiskers are pushed back it will retreat, knowing the rest of its body wouldn't make it through.

2. Birds have whiskers, especially if they are insect eaters. These whiskers, called *rictal bristles*, are used to help scoop up insects while the bird is in flight. Swifts, swallows, and whippoorwills are three different birds with rictal bristles.

3. Fish have whiskers that are tactile; they help them to be more aware of their surroundings.

4. Burrowing insects use their whiskers to help explore their surroundings.

5. On humans, men generally have whiskers on their faces. These whiskers, if allowed to grow, keep the face warmer in cold temperatures. Most women don't have much facial hair, but have an extra layer of fatty tissue compared to men, that helps them remain warm in cold climates.

*Animal
Explorations*

57

MELTED-TEXTURE DRAWING

Texture can be felt in all forms of nature, the bark on a tree, sand on a beach, petals on a flower. A melted-texture drawing allows children to create their own texture design composed of many brilliant colors. Close supervision is required as the children burn candles to melt crayons. The softened crayon creates a rough texture composed of bright colors on the drawing paper. When colors are overlapped and dripped over, new colors and texture designs are created.

Indoor or Outdoor Activity
Time Needed: 30 minutes
Materials Needed: Large selection of crayons for melting, candles, matches, drawing paper, newspaper

1. While on a walk, stop to note the many different textures available in nature. Later, the children will try to create some of these textures with crayon, candle, and paper.
2. Stress safety while working with a burning candle. Do a demonstration before the children begin.
3. Have them draw a rough outline of the shapes they want to color, using a regular crayon.
4. Light the candle and hold a crayon for a few seconds in the flame. Take it immediately to the drawing paper and color with it while it is still melting.
5. Continue this flame-to-paper process to make a textured, colorful drawing. Suggest mixing colors for added effects.

Where Does Wax Come From?

1. *Wax* is defined as being any of various natural, solid, heat-sensitive substances, such as beeswax, consisting essentially of heavy fats.

2. For many years people made the wax candles they used from tallow. *Tallow* is a whitish, tasteless, solid or hard, fat obtained from cattle and sheep. It has also been used in edibles, leather dressing, soap, and lubricants. Most candles of today are made from paraffin, a petroleum product.

Figure 2–10 The worker bee is an amazing wax maker.

3. Bees make wax. In this process the bees eat honey, which is turned into beeswax by special glands. With the spines on their hind legs, they pick up wax scales sticking out from pockets on their abdomens and pass them to their mouths. After they chew and mold the wax into six-sided cells, they build their combs with this beeswax. There are three types of bees—the queen, drone, and worker. The worker bee is the only one to make the wax and only during a certain phase of its short life. Most worker bees live about 38 days and make wax somewhere between their fifteenth and twenty-first days alive. In these perfectly constructed hexagonal cells are laid the eggs, from which later the larvae will mature and emerge.

CUTOUT NATURE SHAPES

A pair of scissors can be used as a drawing tool. Children enjoy the challenge of trying to cut out the shapes of a landscape without having drawn it first. Start with simple shapes, like a mountain, a lake, or clouds. After they have their broad shapes laid down, then smaller shapes will come easier, wildlife, flowers, and trees. Have a large selection of colored construction paper available. This activity can be an individual or group project.

Animal
Explorations

Indoor or Outdoor Activity
Time Needed: 30 minutes
Materials Needed: Variety of colored construction paper, scissors, glue

1. Have the children cut out nature shapes, without using any pencils to draw lines.

2. While the children are cutting out their shapes, have them actually look outdoors for inspiration. They should break away from stereotyped shapes (how one *thinks* a tree looks like) and instead actually look at a tree and then cut out the shape.

3. An assortment of shapes should be cut out and then arranged to create a scene, before gluing anything down. To create depth in the scene, shapes can be put under or in front of other shapes.

How Do Teeth Work to Cut?

1. There are several types of human teeth, each type adapted to perform a different function. There are four incisors on the top and four on the bottom, each used for biting food. The *incisor*

Grasping and Tearing   Gnawing   Rooting   Grazing

Teeth Types

Figure 2–11 Teeth in the animal kingdom perform different functions.

teeth are in front, and the *canines* are the four teeth that border them; both kinds are used for tearing food. The rest of the teeth are called *molars*. Molars are used for grinding, pounding, and crushing food. Children's milk teeth are all lost and replaced by these three kinds of teeth.

2. The teeth of snakes are thin and sharp. Snake teeth usually curve backwards and are used to capture prey, not to break it down. Snakes generally swallow their prey whole.

3. *Carnivorous* (meat-eating) mammals have more pointed teeth than humans. Their teeth are better adapted for cutting and shredding than for grinding.

4. *Herbivores* (grazers) such as deer and sheep have large flat molars with complex ridges and cusps. Often the canine teeth are totally absent in herbivores.

5. Plant eaters have good chewing teeth as they must be able to break down the cell wall, the cellulose, which the plant cells are enclosed in. Cellulose cannot be digested, so animals must be able to chew right through it to get to the foodstuffs. This is why a cow, deer, or any grazer is known to "chew its cud" for long periods of time, as it breaks down the cellulose.

6. Carnivores need not chew their food so laboriously. There are no protective cells in meat, and consequently, carnivores often gulp their food, rarely chewing it at all.

7. Humans are *omnivores* (eat meat and plants) and therefore have teeth adapted to suit both eating purposes.

WEAVINGS FROM NATURE

Simple card weaving is a methodical process. The vertical threads are lifted so the horizontal *weft* threads may be passed over and under the warp alternately to form the weave. Archeologists have found relics of this very process used in basket weaving over 3000 years old. A demonstration using a cardboard hand loom can be shown to the children before they begin working on their own weavings. In this activity, string or yarn should be used for the warp and objects from nature, such as pine needles, grass, or reeds should be used for the weft.

Figure 2–12 Card weavings may have grasses, pine needles, and fibers within them.

Indoor or Outdoor Activity

Time Needed: 1 hour

Materials Needed: Pieces of cardboard (10-in. by 5-in.); string or yarn; scissors; long pencils; old combs; objects from nature such as pine needles, grasses, reeds, or hay

1. On the 5-in. ends of the cardboard cut 10 ½-in. deep notches with the scissors.

2. Knot one end of the string and warp your loom. You do this by beginning with the first notch, running a long piece of string through the notch, allowing the knot to catch in the back. Take that string down the front of the card and catch the first bottom notch. Loop it behind the notch and bring the string back up the front of the card to the second top notch. Loop it behind the second top notch, and again bring it down the front side to the second bottom notch. Continue this process until the front of the card is warped, or has a continuous thread running up and down hooking around the top and bottom notches. Tie and cut the string in the back of the last notch.

3. Take the long pencil and run it across the threads, going under every other warp thread.

4. Lift up the pencil and place a pine needle or grass in this open space.

5. Remove the pencil, then run the pencil again across the threads, this time picking up every other thread that wasn't lifted the first time. Lift up the pencil.

6. Again, place a pine needle or grass in the open space.

7. Repeat the insertion of the pencil over the threads, returning to the threads that were first lifted. Again, place some grass or pine needles in place.

8. After every third weave, take the old comb and "beat" the needles by pushing the woven part toward you, pulling them together tight.

9. Keep up this process until the whole card has been woven.

10. When finished, the weaving may be left on the card or taken off. The threads around the notches are lifted around the front and tied off, so the weaving will stay taut.

How Do Spiders Make a Web?

1. First of all, not all spiders weave webs. Some are hunters, not depending on their webs to catch their food. Some live in the ground or in logs.

Figure 2–13 The spider's web was perhaps the inspiration used by the first human weavers.

2. For the many spiders that do use webs, however, the web is an incredible food trap. The spider has three tubes located at the end of its abdomen, connected to glands within the abdomen. By holding these three tubes together, a thick silk thread is woven, or the spider can weave thin separate threads by leaving them apart.

3. The spider's tubes, or *spinnerets*, are pressed against an object, and then it forces out some of the liquid silk. As the spider moves, more silk is emitted behind it, and the liquid hardens in the air. When the thread is hardened, the spider climbs back up the thread, beginning a second thread. It will do this until it forms a figure like the spokes of a wheel.

4. This spoked wheel is connected with a concentric pattern that the spider begins from the center of the web, working slowly outward and around.

5. Because the spider coats its legs with an oily substance from its mouth, it can travel around on its web without being caught. In a radial web, the spokes are not sticky, only the circular strands are; the spiders get around most of the time on the nonsticky spokes.

SNOW SHELTERS

The forts and clubhouses children build soon become the dwelling places for secret clubs and vivid imaginative play. The child should be credited who can design and build a snow cave that does not cave in, a branch fort that can support a roof, or a mud house that will fit several children. These forts are created by children for "fun" and for a place to call their own. The following activity, snow shelters, will provide fun as well as a safe and surprisingly warm shelter during the winter months.

Outdoor Activity
Time Needed: 2–3 hours
Materials Needed: Shovels, waterproof clothing, snow

1. It's best to have three or four children working on a snow cave. If there is a larger group, there should be several snow caves built.
2. Have the children work where the snow drifts are already built up into mounds. If there are no drifts, make one by shoveling together snow in a pile at least 8 hours before the group is ready to dig, as the pile needs to "set" before being dug into. (It can also be piled up a day or two in advance of the snow-cave digging.)
3. Have the children take turns shoveling out the snow. An entrance tunnel is dug first, 2 to 4 feet long, and only dug high enough for their bodies to be able to slip through.
4. After shoveling and removing the snow from the tunnel, begin to dig the cave itself. The roof needs to stay curved,

CROSS SECTION OF A SNOW CAVE

Figure 2–14 Snow sculptures often have adaptations which make them unique and creative.

and the ceiling thickness should remain consistent for strong support. You can test the thickness with a stick or pole; it should be around 12 inches thick.

5. Digging the cave floor a foot higher than the entrance tunnel's mouth will make it warmer, because the cave chamber is out of a draft. The ceiling should be rubbed smooth with gloves, to alleviate dripping.

What Kinds of Shelters Do Animals Build?

1. Birds build nests for themselves as a part of their reproductive process. Most songbirds, such as canaries, construct their nests in two phases: first, the bowl shape is made in the tree with grasses and twigs; second, the nest is cushioned with added feathers. Nests are made to be comfortable for the female, as she loses many of her feathers on her underside; this is called the "brooding patch." This bare piece of skin is sent an increased amount of blood to enable the mother to keep her eggs warm and is very sensitive to feeling. The feathers cushion her brooding patch.

2. Rodents build tunnels in the ground. The soil composition is a factor determining where they can make their shelters; the soil

cannot be too loose or sandy, or the roots will collapse. These tunnels are of several uses. Some are for sleeping, searching for food, and escaping their predators. Usually the sleeping tunnel is located beneath a boulder or a bush, giving it extra protection against any invaders.

3. Many of the larger mammals—such as mountain lions, coyotes, and bears—have an established den used mainly when the female is raising her young. She may choose a shallow cave, a jumble of fallen logs, or thick brush to hide in. The males rarely spend very much time in the den. Bears enter their deep sleep in a similar hideout. Now determined not to be true hibernators, bears may wake up from their shelter depending on the weather and their food source.

4. Bees build beehives. The worker bees actually construct the hive from beeswax, which they form by a special process of converting honey to a waxy substance. There are as many as 20,000 to 40,000 bees in an individual hive, living and working together.

HAND PUPPETS FROM NATURE

Hand puppets made from materials found in the children's neighborhood provide a creative activity, and they can plan a puppet show to display them. Moss and cornsilk can be used for hair, sticks can be tied together to form bodies, and ferns and feathers can form the clothes. The puppet's head can be made from clay with pebbles and seeds forming the facial features. After making the puppets, the next step is to find a stage. Outdoors, this could be a large boulder, a fallen tree, or two trees with a blanket tied between them; indoors, a large desk or countertop will do. With the puppets and stage prepared, have the children perform a show for their friends and families.

Indoor or Outdoor Activity
Time Needed: 1–2 hours
Materials Needed: Collection of nature objects (such as sticks, moss, seeds, feathers, leaves, clay, seashells), string, glue, fabric scraps, scissors

Figure 2–15 Hand puppets can be made from sticks, shells, feathers, and mosses.

1. Have a large collection of nature objects gathered so the children's imaginations will be triggered to make their puppets.

2. A body can be built on a cross framework, with two sticks crossing each other and tied together with a piece of string.

3. Mold the head out of clay and attach the cornsilk or moss to it. A hat could be made from a leaf or a shell. Small pebbles or seeds can form the facial features.

4. Tie or glue the pine needles, feathers, fabric scraps, or ferns on for clothes.

5. Have the bottom of the stick longer than the top, making a handle to hold the puppet from under the stage.

Do Animals Have Certain Ways of Acting?

1. Most animals act certain ways when they are hungry, during mating times, when the seasonal changes prompt the need for

shelter or travel, and when threatened. Animals and people have many ways of acting that are learned behavior and others that are instinctual. Yet, just like people, the animal kingdom has unique individuals who have unusual ways of acting.

2. Similar to people, some animals stay at home year-round; others travel with the season. Animals who do not migrate usually have a good local food supply and a mild climate. Those who travel usually do so because of seasonal shortages of food, local overpopulations, or the need to avoid severe weather.

3. Some animals do not migrate but *emigrate*. Emigrants leave their home territory and do not return. The main reason for this behavior is increasing competition in the original habitat. If a population grows too large there is less food available, so animals tend to move to find new food sources. In the United States, the grey squirrel is frequently on the move from one food source to another.

4. Humans are a frequent cause of this emigration of different species. When the animals' habitat—whether land, trees, ponds, or ocean—is taken away and developed or polluted, the species either perishes or moves away.

5. Many animals who live in severe climates do not leave but hibernate instead. They retire to the underground world or stay hidden away in trees during the late fall or early winter, sleeping through the cold months. Some are not "true hibernators" in that they wake up from time to time, such as the bear, skunk, and oppossum. But true hibernators, like frogs, woodchucks, and ground squirrels, undergo such physiological changes in their bodily functions that they appear almost dead. When a ground squirrel hibernates, its heartbeat may change from 300 beats per minute to 5, and its temperature may be just a couple of degrees above freezing.

TWELVE-INCH HIKE

We often get visually swept up in the larger elements of outdoor scenery, whether it be a river, ocean, or mountain. The smaller features of a landscape get less attention and, therefore, seem to lack in significance. The Twelve-inch Hike is an exercise to encourage

Figure 2–16 The insects, sand, and driftwood take on special importance through a twelve-inch hike.

awareness of the fascinating world right beneath the children's feet. The child is equipped with pencil and paper and asked to draw anything he or she notices in a single 12-in. square of earth. The grasses, insect world, and soil become a vivid part of the outdoor scenery through this drawing exercise.

Outdoor Activity
Time Needed: 15–30 minutes
Materials Needed: Paper, pencil, drawing boards

1. Have the children spread out over an open area where they can sit quietly alone for 15 minutes.
2. During this time, ask the children to mentally mark off a square foot. Have them begin to draw whatever they see in their marked area.
3. Encourage them to include any insect life that may crawl or buzz by their area. Have them try to copy the complex-

ity of the patterns of grasses. Mention the soil's texture and color and how it should be included in their drawing.

4. After the 15 minutes have passed, assemble the group and ask them to share what they noticed and drew.

How Do Insects Hear and See?

1. Few insects have hearing organs located on their heads. Instead their ears, or tympanic organs, are located in various parts of their bodies. In the grasshopper and cricket, they are found on the tibia of each foreleg. In the cicada, they are found on the bottom of the abdomen. Moths' tympanic organs are located on either side of the rear of the thorax or the front part of the abdomen. This thin membrane vibrates when sound waves strike it, and the vibrations are passed on to the auditory nerve. Through the auditory nerve, sound is detected within the brain.

2. Most insects have tiny hairs that react to sound vibrations in the air. Sometimes these hairs are found on the antennae, sometimes all over the body, as in some caterpillars.

3. Most insects do not hear sound as well as humans. Although it is a difficult thing to measure, many insects hear sound frequencies different from the human range.

4. Most insects have two forms of vision, a pair of large compound eyes and a number of small, simple eyes or *ocelli*. The ocelli act to distinguish light from dark. The compound eye is responsible for perceiving a degree of form perception, depth perception, and color awareness. Most caterpillars only have ocelli, and therefore their vision is minimal, seeing one or two inches in front of them.

5. Insects cannot focus their vision, and distant objects are blurred. Since, at a distance, moving objects are easier to detect, remaining still will keep a wasp or bee from coming close and stinging.

6. Some worker ants are blind. Many insects who live entirely in dark caves or under the earth's surface have poor vision, if any at all.

ANIMAL TRACK DISCOVERY

After close examination, animal tracks can often be found outside, whether in sand, mud, or snow. These tracks make good investigative clues for children to follow and to eventually identify what animal made them. The children can reproduce the tracks either by drawing them on paper or making prints themselves in earth. An animal's size, speed, and seasonal habits may be discovered through the study of its tracks. Discuss with the group what the animal was doing or where it was going. These discoveries give the children more insight into the animal's habitats.

Outdoor Activity
Time Needed: Open
Materials Needed: Paper, pencil

1. On an outing, have the group explore for animal tracks. The best place to find tracks of animals such as deer, squirrels, birds, raccoons, coyotes, beaver, or mice is near a river, stream, or creek bank.

2. Once a track is found, mark a circle around it so it will be obvious for the whole group to see. Have the children try to reproduce the track with their fingers in the dirt or snow.

3. Encourage them to sketch any tracks that are observed. The drawings are done to keep a record of the animals found in that location, and for the children to be able to identify the tracks for themselves in the future.

Animal Hooves Versus Paws

1. Most animals bearing paws with claws are carnivores. Hunters, they are dependent on the ability to stalk quietly and capture their prey. Examples of animals with paws and claws are the cat family, bears, raccoons, and coyotes.

2. Those animals with hooves are herbivores. They graze on various plants in their habitat. These hooves are used to break through ground surfaces, for balance, and for defense. Examples of animals with hooves are deer, sheep, horses, and elk.

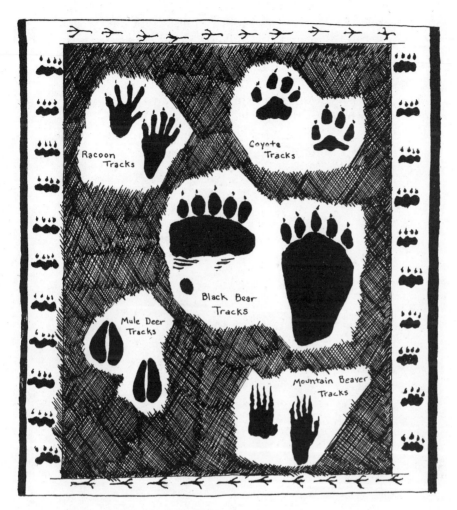

Figure 2–17 Drawing animal tracks will help teach animal identification.

3. Many of the pawed animals are known for their ability to climb trees, stalk their prey, and manipulate their paws as if they had a thumb similar to humans. Cats are known to be able to open doors, bears will get into picnic baskets, and raccoons will hold their prey near the stream. None of these animals' paws have quite the dexterity of the human hand, but combined with their mouths and perseverance, they are able to use their paws in amazing ways.

4. Hooved animals are known for speed, grace, and in some cases climbing abilities. Mountain sheep and mountain goats have

some of the greatest known climbing abilities for a large mammal; they can perch themselves on ledges where wolves and bears cannot follow them.

5. Some of the clawed animals use different strategies in stalking their prey. Cats don't show their claws except when using them, while those in the dog family always have their claws exposed. Dogs use traction and speed for their hunting, while cats use stealth and quietness to catch their food.

People and Places 3

The beauty of this country is becoming part of me.
Everett Ruess
A Vagabond for Beauty

People's artwork is a reflection of their environment. Climatic changes, the abundance of food and water, and the availability of leisure time affect the culture within a geographic area. Throughout history, where weather, soil, and water have allowed agriculture to develop, people have stayed in one place, and with that stability, art developed.

Nomadic people had art in their lives, exhibited in their decorative dance rituals, hunting tools, and clothes. But, with agriculture, time became available to develop sculpture, painting, and architecture. The study of art history reveals how civilization slowly emerged from the world of nature. During this evolution, people have reflected their views of the natural world through art.

Art is built on a foundation deriving from nature. Landscapes, seascapes, wildlife, plants, and people are subjects often found in paintings and sculptures. Nature's images have been widely interpreted during this century. With abstract and symbolic artwork, nature has been used as an inspiration instead of a direct interpretation. The power of a thunderstorm, the vastness of the open desert, and the calmness of a summer's evening are examples of nature interpretation that inspires art. The feelings nature promotes have been explored, but also, the shapes, colors, and textures are evident in today's artwork. Every hue, pattern, or form found in paintings, commercial designs, or sculptures have their origin in nature. As a civilization moves further away from the land, art, with its influence from nature, serves to connect people with their ancestry. Art reflects who we are and where we came from.

People are a part of nature. It is a recent misconception that we are separate from it. This chapter offers activities for you to help the children understand their relationship to other people and how to interpret their environment. Through nature jewelry and wall hangings, they will experience how people decorated themselves and their homes. Learning to keep a sketchbook will help them realize they can interpret nature in their own style. Their sketchbook should be their picture diary in which they can dream and draw. The trace-hand environment activity is one which shows how the symbols of their world can be related to others all over the world. To know we live intricately connected to nature is an important concept for the children to grasp. Use these thoughts and activities to help the children feel their association with others on the planet.

GROUP MURAL

After a recent outing, a group mural is an exciting way for children to express their memories of the trip. The highlights of the outing can be incorporated into one large drawing. A large piece of butcher paper, felt-tip markers, and crayons are adequate materials to make an expressive mural. With permission from the neighborhood, a group drawing can also be put on a local wall, blank wall, or construction fence using paints and brushes. Excellent for group cohesiveness, this activity encourages all to participate and communicate with each other. A mural may also be an individual project, allowing a child to gather together many memories from the outing and draw them on one large sheet of paper.

Indoor or Outdoor Activity
Time Needed: 30 minutes to 1 hour (to design the mural on paper with markers and crayons—longer to paint on a fence or wall)
Materials Needed: Large sheets of butcher paper (7-ft. by 3-ft. approximately), felt-tip markers, crayons, flat surface for drawing

1. Have the children discuss their memories of a recent outing.
2. Divide the group so that there are no more than eight children per mural, or increase the size of the paper. Every child should participate in some of the mural.
3. Have the children illustrate their highlights of a recent outing. They should discuss it first, perhaps incorporating a theme, or they could create a mural composed of scattered pictures of their trip.
4. Present and display the murals so the whole group and their friends may enjoy them.

What Were Some of the First Murals?

1. Some of the earliest and most famous examples of early mural art are found in Europe. The French caves at Lascaux are the best known of the many prehistoric sites in that country. History

Figure 3–2 A mural gets the whole group talking, planning and drawing.

interaction of the children

2. The Lascaux caves were discovered by accident in 1940 by some boys whose dog had fallen into a hole; that hole led to a chamber of primitive art work. All of the animal images were to be found deep within the cave, hidden away from the elements and intruders.

3. Archeologists date the cave paintings by a process called *radiocarbon dating*. According to this method, the art found in Lascaux is believed to be from 15,000 to 13,000 B.C.

4. The images are of animals that were hunted: bison, deer, horses, and cattle. Portrayed naturalistically from a sideview, the animal figures are racing across the walls and ceilings in wild profusion, some only in a black outline and other filled in with bright earth colors.

5. The people who made these murals are called the Magdalenians. The art is believed to be linked with certain hunting rituals. Two theories speculate as to why the Magdalenians made pictures to accompany their hunting: it was either a magic ritual that would ensure a successful kill or it was meant to magically attract more animals in their area. Depicted with the animals are also spears and traps, showing how these people hunted.

STENCIL DRAWING

Stencils can be used in repetition to create a design on walls, fabric, paper, or any art work. A stencil can also be used as a special signature representing the designer. This symbol is first sketched onto a piece of paper, then, using an X-Acto knife or mat blade, the design is cut out. It is the negative space that will be used as the stencil. The children should design their own stencils; the designing and the cutting out are important parts of this activity. Stencils may be reused many times. Stress safety with the knife blade during this activity.

Indoor or Outdoor Activity
Time Needed: 30 minutes
Materials Needed: X-Acto knife or scissors, pencils, paper, tempera paint, brush, watercolor paper

1. Have the children draw a symbol design that they feel will make a good stencil and that will represent themselves. Simple nature shapes work well—for example, shapes of a daisy, a pine tree, or a butterfly. Draw the symbol on paper. Cut the shape out with scissors or a knifeblade.

2. Lay the cutout shape on the top of thick paper, such as watercolor paper, which will be the stencil. Draw around the cutout shape and cut very carefully to form the stencil.

3. To print, tape the stencil to the surface that will be printed.

4. The tempera paint should be mixed to a thick consis-

Figure 3–3 Making stencils develops the children's skills in drawing, cutting, and painting.

tency. Brush it over the entire stencil. Do not lift up until it is completely dry. Lift it gently off the paper.

5. The stencil may be used several times, using the same or other colors.

Early Cutting Tools

1. Early people all over the planet found resources close at hand to use for cutting tools. As these early cultures evolved, people traded their resources for distant tools that were even better for cutting, spearing, and hunting prey. Of course, the most basic cutting tool was the people's own teeth: Sharp canines could tear meat, and molars could chew it.

2. Shells, bones, and sharp rocks that were found became tools and were traded in order to cut and mold other tools.

*People
and Places*

3. *Flint* is a hard quartz that sparks when struck with steel. A rock, when sharpened, was used for arrowheads and spear points.

4. *Obsidian* is an acid-resistant, lustrous, volcanic, glasslike rock. It can be shaped and broken to a very fine edge, as sharp as glass, which makes a fine cutting tool. Obsidian originates from the most rapid cooling of lava, leaving the mineral black, shiny and smooth.

5. Indians in many areas used obsidian in the making of their arrowheads. These points were attached directly to the end of the arrow by sinew (a tendon) lashings, and sticky pitch (from the trees). The arrows were made usually from either willows or alders.

6. The obsidian or flint was flaked from a core rock by hitting it with a larger stone, called a hammerstone. The flake was then chipped with an antler tool, from a deer. The material for the arrowhead was grasped in the palm of the hand, which was protected by a leather pad; this pad kept the hand from being cut by the sharp flakes. The flaking by the antler tool was laborious, a skill that often the elderly men knew much better than the young boys. Women did not make arrowheads.

JEWELRY FROM NATURE

The adornment of human bodies with nature jewelry is an ancient art. Belts made from woodpecker scalps, necklaces from abalone shells, or ankle bracelets made of bones are examples of early jewelry. A child may make many simple constructions to wear. A necklace made from collected shells, glued acorns, or even split peas will teach children creativity and patience. Designs can be simple, such as repeating corn kernels, or as beautiful and intricate as a shell, feather, and bead necklace. The children enjoy searching in their local areas for feathers, rocks with holes in them, shells, or other items appropriate for decorative jewelry.

Indoor or Outdoor Activity
Time Needed: 1 hour
Materials Needed: String or fishing line, objects from nature, strong needles, dried split peas or corn kernels.

Figure 3–4 Woven grasses, seed pods on a string, and a favorite seashell will provide nature jewelry.

1. After discussing "early jewelry" (mention feather earrings, beaded necklaces, woven grass bracelets), go for a walk looking for items to make jewelry with.

2. Assemble all the findings. Have the string, fishing line, scissors, glue, and needles at hand. Let the children decide what they are going to make. Have them cut the appropriate length of string.

3. Encourage them to think of their design before they begin their construction. It is a good idea to use one or two of the most prominent found objects (such as an especially colorful shell or feather) and then surround them with beads made from glued peas, corn, or berries.

4. To fill the string, have them glue their peas on the thread or thread the corn kernels on with a needle.

5. To soften the corn for stringing, put two cups of corn with two cups of water on the stove. Allow it to boil, then simmer for 15 minutes. If the corn is to be dyed a color, add a ½ cup of dye right in with the water. Remove the pan from the heat, and let the corn stand in the dye and water for 10 more minutes. Rinse under cool water and

pierce with a darning needle and thimble immediately, before the corn dries and hardens again.

How Did the Indians Get Their Jewelry?

1. There were (and are today) hundreds of different Native American tribes across the American continent. Each of these different tribes has particular features in their culture and their jewelry that make them unique.

2. Feathers, bones, stones, and metals from local areas were often the foundation of many different types of jewelry. Different people, both men and women, would pierce their ears and noses to decorate their bodies.

3. Oftentimes, jewelry would be a major source of trade. Inland Indians would trade foodstuffs for beautiful abalone shells as well as beads brought to this country from far-off lands. The blue glass beads especially treasured by Native Americans came from Russia.

4. Beautiful combs to be worn in the hair often were carved from cows' and horses' hooves.

5. Some of the beads that the Indians wore were local. They were carved from shells, bones, and made out of ceramics and fired in kilns.

6. The Indians of the Southwest love silver and turquoise. In the Navajo society women that wore the most jewelry owned the most property. The women were the weavers as well.

FABRIC WALL HANGING

Appliqué is a kind of cloth collage made up of pieces of cloth composing a pattern or picture and sewn onto a background of fabric. Scissors, thread and needles, and fabric scraps are the art tools in this activity. The children each compose a square to add to the groups' large wall hanging. Each square should reflect a memory from a recent outing: a trip to the ocean, the desert, a local hilltop, or a nearby farm. If everyone contributes, the variety in the wall hanging should be colorful and interesting.

Figure 3–5 A fabric wall hanging gets the whole group involved.

Indoor or Outdoor Activity
Time Needed: Several hours
Materials Needed: Needles, thread, 8-in. by 8-in. squares of fabric, scissors, cloth scraps (felt works great)

1. This is a group activity; each person will design a square or several squares to compose a wall hanging.

2. The design of the squares should be based on a group outdoor experience, whether it be to the mountains, the zoo, the local park, or pond.

3. Have the children first design their square on a sheet of paper. Have them cut the paper into patterns and trace the shapes onto the fabric scraps. Cut out the shapes and design them on the square before beginning to sew.

People and Places

85

4. Let them stitch their square using any color of thread that pleases them. Some squares can have the appliqued pieces stuffed with cotton for added relief.

5. Sew these squares onto a solid color background, with each square being placed several inches from the others.

6. Hang the finished wall hanging on display for all the children to see.

What Did the Indians Use to Sew?

1. Many Native Americans used sinew—ligaments that attach muscle to bone—for a version of thread and needles made of bone with which to sew. They would use these sewing tools when they were attaching animal skins together to make blankets, moccasins, and winter clothes. The leather would be poked with a sharp tool, such as a deer antler, to form a hole that the sinew could be pulled through.

2. In the Southwest many of the people were weavers and spinners. They raised the sheep, spun their wool, and would weave fabric. This fabric would then be sewn to make clothes, rugs, and blankets.

3. West Coast Indians used a tule grass, or small bulrush, which they broke off from the stalks with sharp flints or their fingernails. They then bleached, and wove them into breechcloths.

4. Milkweed was used to make string, cord, and nets. The inner bark was dried, then crushed by the Indians' teeth. Sometimes the bark was stripped and the milkweed core was twisted into strands and very fine thread.

5. Many of the blankets for men and women were made from the skins of various animals, such as the deer, bear, mountain lion, buffalo, and coyote. The most common for the West Coast Indians were those made by winding narrow strips of rabbit skin about milkweed cords to form a loose but warm blanket.

6. Indian hemp was also used to make nets, string, and cord. The people would gather this stalklike plant and roll and twist the fibers into a strong string.

SKETCHBOOK-JOURNAL

A sketchbook can be a great tool for recording memories and improving one's writing and drawing skills. With a sketchbook-journal, a child can record not only what he sees around him, but also what he is thinking. The sketchbook-journal helps children develop a personal creative tool; its empty white pages can be filled with the children's reflections on their colorful lives. They should be encouraged to draw and write in it any time—not only after a trip outdoors, but also while waiting for the bus, during slow periods of school, and while at home.

Indoor or Outdoor Activity
Time Needed: 30 minutes/1 hour
Materials Needed: Purchase a spiral-bound drawing book, fabric of child's choice, clear acetate paper, scissors, glue, pressed flowers, or favorite drawing

1. Have the children cut a piece of fabric to cover the front and back cover of the sketchbook-journal. Have them glue the fabric down carefully.

2. On the inside front flap have the children arrange either pressed flowers or a favorite drawing and glue them down. A favorite quotation or saying would be nice also.

3. Cover both the fabric and the inside flaps with clear acetate paper. This will adhere to the surfaces as well as protect them from moisture.

4. The aim of this activity is for the child to make such a special sketchbook-journal that he or she will enjoy taking it along almost anywhere to draw.

Why Did John Muir Keep a Sketchbook-Journal?

1. John Muir (1883–1914) was a naturalist, a poet, a geologist, a conservationist, a writer, a botanist, a philosopher, and he had many other titles as well. His life's work was to understand nature as much as he could, and to foster that appreciation in others. Be-

Figure 3–6 A sketchbook can become a favorite possession to take outdoors.

cause of his efforts thousands of acres of land were set aside, to remain undeveloped and open for people, animals, plants, and rivers to run free. He kept a sketchbook-journal for several reasons.

a. Sketchbook-journals allowed him to chronicle his adventures. People didn't have portable cameras, and small sketches provided visual memories of the land he saw.

b. Sketchbook-journals, always at hand, allowed John Muir to record thoughts and ideas that were spontaneous expressions. Oftentimes, if he hadn't written down his spontaneous thoughts, they would have been lost forever.

c. Muir used these journals to refer back to when writing magazine articles, books, and letters. Because of his efforts, people of today have become more interested in nature and adventure in the out-of-doors. He also became financially successful through his writings.

d. Finally, these sketchbook-journals have become very valuable in the historical sense; they are carefully written and illustrated records of natural environments and changes in them.

BAMBOO WIND CHIMES

Children listening to the sounds of wind-blown chimes they have made themselves gain a new appreciation for the sounds created by nature. These wind chimes can be constructed from bamboo cuttings, nails, cut pipes, glass pieces, or many other found objects. The children's creativity is utilized in deciding what the chimes will be made of, how they will be held together, and where they should hang. Each different object will have a unique sound.

Indoor or Outdoor Activity
Time Needed: 1 hour
Materials Needed: Bamboo (as available), small handsaw, hand drill, fishing line

1. In gathering the bamboo, pick up the dried yellow pieces, not the moist green stalks. Check for hollowness. The most hollow stalks will make the nicest sounds.

2. The best lengths to saw are between 8 and 16 inches.

Figure 3–7
Bamboo is a material used to make wind chimes.

3. Cut eight to twelve pieces.

4. Carefully drill holes at the tops of the bamboo pieces.

5. The bamboo will hang from another long top piece or from a round rim. Drill holes in this piece every half inch.

6. Tie the fishing line from the bamboo pieces to the top holder.

7. Tie a secure, balanced piece of fishing line connecting the entire wind chime to a ceiling or a tree branch.

8. Making the bamboo chime is just one way in which children may experiment with sounds through wind chimes.

How Do We Hear Sound?

1. Our hearing device actually consists of three divisions: the outer ear, the middle ear, and the inner ear.

2. The outer ear's main function is to catch the sound. Ani-

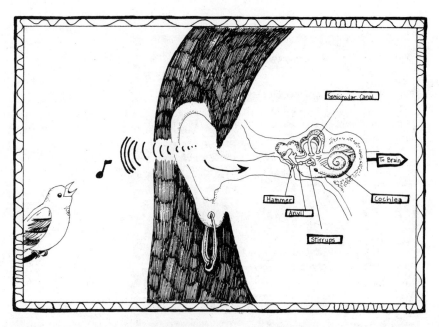

Figure 3–8 This diagram illustrates how we hear sound.

mals' ears raise up when listening carefully, to catch as much sound as possible. These trapped vibrations are then sent down the auditory canal to the eardrum. This eardrum is a membrane that vibrates when the sound waves strike it.

3. Behind the eardrum is the middle ear. This area is hollow except for three small connected bones. They are called the hammer, anvil, and stirrup. They are connected to each other as well as the eardrum and the rear wall of the middle ear. When the car drum vibrates, these bones are set in motion.

4. This motion is carried into the inner ear. Within this final compartment is the cochlea, a snaillike compartment filled with liquid and the ends of hearing nerves. These nerve endings send the vibrations through the auditory nerve and to the front part of the brain, called the cerebrum. In the cerebrum is the hearing center of the brain. The message is received and the sounds are recognized.

BROKEN GLASS MOSAIC

Recycled litter, in the form of broken glass, can create a beautiful mosaic piece. Glass bottles can be separated by color in metal garbage cans and broken down into small pieces. These pieces will be used for mosaics. Use gloves and tweezers when working with the broken glass pieces. Stress safety.

Indoor or Outdoor Activity
Time Needed: 1 hour, plus collecting time
Materials Needed: plaster of paris, grout, broken glass, metal trash cans, gloves, tweezers, cutoff milk containers in which to pour plaster

1. Have a litter pickup. Let the children know they are looking especially for glass. The best places to find bottles are in alleys, along roads, and near trash dumpsters.
2. Separate the bottles by color in different metal trash cans. Carefully break up the bottles.

People and Places

91

Figure 3–9 Beautiful results can occur in a glass mosaic when safety is used.

3. Pour the glass bits into different milk cartons, separating them by color.

4. Prepare the plaster of paris in the other milk cartons.

5. Have the children wear gloves and pick out the pieces of glass with tweezers. Have them arrange a composition of glass in the wet plaster of paris.

6. After the plaster sets with the glass arranged in it, mix up the grout mixture according to the directions. Pour the grout over the mosaic to smooth out the surface of the glass pieces. Rub the mosaic with a dry rag after the grout has dried.

7. These mosaics make fine gifts, to be hung on the wall or set on a desk or table.

Where Does Glass Come From?

1. Glass is an artificial substance formed by the joining of fine materials, such as sand, with some alkali. There are as many recipes for making glass as there are for making cookies, but sand and alkali are the two main ingredients usually used.

2. Alkali comes in the form of potash and carbonate of soda or lime. When the alkali is greatly heated it causes the fusion of the materials.

3. Glass has peculiar properties. When in its liquid state, it is like molasses in January and can be molded and spun and given countless shapes. Glass can be crystal clear or, by adding metallic oxides, can be any color of the rainbow. The only acid that affects it is hydrofluoric. Though often very fragile, glass can also be made bulletproof and heat-resistant.

4. Glass is believed to have first been discovered in ancient Syria. Glassmaking became a highly developed art utilizing the sand from the region of Belus. The Egyptian culture also made glass very early in its civilization. The Romans in the first century A.D. were great glass makers: they made glass mosaics, crystal, and glass molds. The Roman empire spread the art of glassmaking for a great distance, encouraging glass to become a household article.

5. Today glass enters our lives in many ways. Imagine what homes would be like without glass windows, mirrors, or light bulbs. Glass has enabled the astronomer's telescope to explore the heavens, and the microscopic worlds of land and water to be discovered. The study of medicine and chemistry continues to grow with the aid of glass.

6. Glass art in tableware and ornamental pieces is treasured for its beauty of form, color, and decoration. Glass is a link in the craftworld from antiquity to the present.

IMAGINATIVE SAND DWELLINGS

This activity takes children beyond simple sand-castle building. Build a whole community in the sand, and one with environmental planning in mind. In their sand creations they should be thinking what natural resources are needed—such as a forest, lake, or river—where agriculture areas are, where people should live, and where and why there should be uninhabited areas. If the children begin their sand building with environmental planning in mind, they may begin to see a need for future planning in their own worlds.

Outdoor Activity
Time Needed: 30 minutes
Materials Needed: Sand

1. Sand piles are accessible near the shores of many streams, lakes, and the ocean. Also, one can find sand in a schoolyard play area, near construction sites, and in local parks.

2. Once at the sand area, talk with the children about how their local environment provides for food, water, shelter, sanitation, recreation, and education.

3. Have the children, either individually or in groups, build in the sand an imaginary environment that provides for these needs.

Figure 3–10
Building a community in the sand takes group effort and design.

4. Have them explain where their sand environment's water comes from, where the wild places are, and what kind of vegetation grows there.

What Makes a Community?

1. A *community* in the biological sense is when all the organisms are living together in a certain environment and affecting one another in various ways. For example, a forest of trees and undergrowth plants, inhabited by animals and rooted in soil containing bacteria and fungi, constitutes a biological community.

2. Important elements of a community that must be included, and are as vital as the plants and animals, are sunlight, moisture, and air.

3. A community is only complete when it is self-sustaining, not dependent on anyone or anything bringing in additional elements or taking away from it. All biological communities have carnivores (meat eaters), herbivores (plant eaters), and bacteria (decomposers) to make it complete.

4. In a community everyone and everything has a defined role and job, called its "niche."

5. Just as there are functioning communities of people in neighborhoods, towns, states, and countries, there are biological communities found in the forest, the desert, the ocean, and under your own porch steps.

LITTER SCULPTURE

Waste is a human concept. What we call "trash" can be reused in many ways. Glass, paper, and metal can be recycled to form new things—one of which is art. Many forms, textures, and shapes of discarded objects can be used to make sculpture. Used fruit crates, old bottles, aluminum foil, old shoe leather, colored paper—many such discards can be viewed by children as materials for their sculpture activity. A litter pickup project, for example, may turn up a gold mine of sculpture materials, as well as clean up the local area.

Indoor or Outdoor Activity
Time Needed: 1 hour
Materials Needed: "Found litter" (not to be taken from trash cans),
glue, string, tacks, scissors

1. Have the children go out with large plastic bags and pick up litter in a needed area. Have them dump their found objects and examine them. Make sure they notice the texture in carpet scraps, the shine of aluminum cans, or the labels on wooden fruit crates.

2. Children can work in a group if they wish. Each sculpture should be at least 2 feet high. Encourage the children to hang objects one from another. Try to have them use metal, wood, and fabric scraps together, assembling their sculptures using the string, glue, tacks, and scissors. An example: take metal cans and smash them flat; assemble them with a cardboard box supported on old bed springs.

3. Arrange to display the sculptures in the area where the trash was picked up—whether it be the school, the shop-

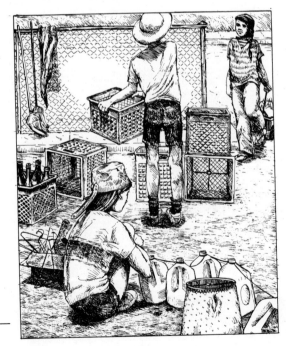

Figure 3–11 Discarded plastic containers and old bottles can be collected to assemble litter sculpture.

ping center, or the fire station—to show how the children are concerned about littering in the area. These displays also show how "trash" can be recycled in an art form.

Why Is Waste a Human Concept?

1. Everything in nature is recycled. That is, everything is always becoming something else. When a tree dies, it decomposes with the help of fungi, insects, and weather, and becomes soil in which new growth will occur.

2. People add things to the environment that are not easily recycled. For example plutonium, used in nuclear power reactors, is an extremely radioactive element and cannot properly be returned to the environment for thousands and thousands of years. Plutonium has become a waste product, as people can find no use for it after it leaves the nuclear power plants.

3. Animal waste, or *scat*, is not thought of as waste in an animal's habitat. Animals track one another and mark their territory with their urine. Their scat returns to the soil, enriching it in return. Humans are the only terrestrial animals who put their waste in water. We defecate into toilets, which use water as a method of transportation to carry the waste matter to either treatment plants or into our oceans or lakes. No animals contaminate their water with their scat or urine, only people do it regularly, believing that by flushing it away, it goes to a safe place. In China, the people recycle their "wastes" to enrich their soil, careful not to lose this natural resource.

4. Recycling stations are becoming more popular around the country. It is now possible in most cities and towns to return used newspaper, glass, and metal to recycling centers. Our natural resources are limited. We should not regard them as waste, but let them be used over and over, as in nature.

TRACE-HAND ENVIRONMENT

The "trace-hand" activity encourages children to realize and then illustrate some of their favorite environments. The child's hand is placed flat on a piece of drawing paper and then traced. Within this familiar tracing, separate drawings are done inside the palm tracing, the thumb, and each of the fingers in response to questions about favorite environments. By illustrating some of their favorite places and objects in nature, the children will develop a personalized picture of what they want their world to look like.

Indoor or Outdoor Activity
Time Needed: 20 minutes
Materials Needed: Paper, pencils, colors

1. Discuss with the group what the term "environment" means. A dictionary definition would be: "A combination of internal and external conditions that affect the growth and development of living things." Have the children give examples of what their favorite environment would be.

2. Have everyone trace his hand onto a sheet of paper with a favorite color.

3. In the palm have them draw with a pencil a picture of their favorite environment.

4. Have them be prepared to answer five questions by drawing a picture in each of the fingers. Some questions might be: What is their favorite tree? Season? Flower? Animal? Favorite part of their body? The group may want to suggest their own questions to illustrate.

Why Is Art Called a "Universal Language"?

1. Art is called a "universal language" because it uses symbols to represent what is seen or felt rather than a specific language or vocabulary. People from all over the world and throughout time have used similar symbols to draw the sun, water, or four-legged animals. Paintings done by a German-speaking person, for example, can be appreciated by people from any other culture, no matter what language they speak. The artist's best method of explaining his or her work is not in words but rather by making the art available to be seen by as many people as possible.

2. People from all over the world have been understood through their art work. Pottery dating back thousands of years

helps to explain how a different civilization lived and prospered. Modern cultures from different parts of the world are studied and represented through their costumes, dances, rituals, basketry, and other art forms.

3. People who interpret their environment through art are not only making pictures of their friends and surroundings, but also interpreting the meaning of the times in which they live. Art work often lives on after the artist dies, and the times that the artist captured are retained for others of the future.

4. The artist's purpose is not to draw nature exactly as it is seen, but rather to do as nature does, to create anew. The artist takes inspiration from nature and invents something new, a private creation.

STORY ILLUSTRATION

Reading to a child stirs up vivid pictures in the young person's mind. The activity of story illustration involves having children illustrate the story read to them. The children can help select the fairy tale, folk tale, or Indian legend. A story involving the wilderness or the outdoors should invoke vivid pictures in the children's imaginations. Determining the climax of the story will help determine which scene should be illustrated. By illustrating the story as they hear it, it is probable that the story will stay with the children longer.

Indoor or Outdoor Activity
Time Needed: 1 hour
Materials Needed: Reading material, drawing paper, drawing tools, drawing boards

1. Be selective about your reading material. Visit the local library and assemble a collection of books. Have material that is vivid and descriptive, and offers a view of the outside world. *Select a fairy tale or other children's story that has a vivid description*
2. Allow the children to be in comfortable listening positions. Let them know before reading that they will be asked to do a drawing.

The children must know beforehand that they are to do a drawing afterward

Figure 3–12 While drawing symbols for favorite things the children may learn more about themselves.

3. Let them make sketches during the reading, but encourage the children to wait until the story is finished before they draw their final illustration.

4. Have the children display their drawings afterward. It is very interesting to see how differently each child can picture the same character or landscape.

Allow the children to sketch ideas during the story but the final drawing should wait until the end of the story

Recommended Readings

1. Stories involving goblins, witches, fairies, and princes seem to often take place in forests, by rivers, or near the ocean. Adults and children alike have their favorite story books that they love to hear read aloud to evoke images of the natural world. Reading these beautiful imaginative stories out loud to the children,

whether they are by Hans Christian Andersen, the Brothers Grimm, or Mother Goose, is a timeless and wonderful activity.

2. Story books and fairy tales are not the only rich sources of natural images for children. There are many large picture books (not always in the children's section of the library) that supply wonderful images of the outside world. Picture books on animals, plants, mountains, the planets, stars, rivers, and the different continents are great for youngsters to hear read aloud. In the library's card catalog, look up Natural History under the subject category; there you will find listed scores of fantastic books for reading and drawing.

3. Certain authors write much about the natural world. Some names to keep in mind in your library search are Edward Abbey, Jack London, Mark Twain, Ray Bradbury, Henry David Thoreau, Peter Matthiessen, and Annie Dillard. Some poets who include the outside world in their poems are Walt Whitman, Robert Frost, Robert Service, and Gary Snyder.

4. Read aloud *The Dark Range* by David Rains Wallace (published by the Sierra Club), which describes the habits of wildlife at night.

Figure 3–13 Children love to have books read to them.

5. For great adventure stories about the outdoors read from *The World of Farley Mowat* by Peter Davidson (Little, Brown, 1980). Another book is *Adventures in the Wilderness* by Rutherford Platt (American Heritage Publishing Company, 1963).

6. Books with lasting visual images of the seasonal changes are *Wilderness Days* by Sigurd F. Olson (Knopf, 1972), *One Day on Beetle Rock* by Sally Carrighar (Knopf, 1944), and *Sand County Almanac* by Aldo Leopold (Oxford University Press, 1949).

7. Some books can be read aloud to children. Others can be read alone by the adult first, to inspire a story told aloud, or a walk in the wilderness. Some books in this category include *The Sense of Wonder* by Rachel Carson (Harper & Row, 1965), and *The Zen of Seeing* by Frederick Franck (Vintage Books, 1973).

Earth
Science 4

The real laws of art, the basic laws, are few. These basic laws are the laws of nature. They existed even before the first drawing was made.
Kimon Nicolaides
The Natural Way to Draw

The forces which allow plants, animals, and people to exist on earth are mysteries, still being unraveled. Soil, sunlight, water, gravity, fire, and our atmosphere are fundamental for life to thrive on earth. These factors allow each of us to breathe, eat, reproduce, and be comfortable, although most of us rarely acknowledge our dependency. When one is dependent upon something, it is usually made easily available; when things are easy to find they are often taken for granted. These powerful forces have been with us all our lives, yet we rarely take the time to understand them.

Everything becomes more precious to us when we fear that we may lose it. Air, water, and soil are limited resources which we must learn to think of as being precious. Rising prices of declining resources and the media's promotion of conservation help to curb the overuse of limited natural resources, but there is a more effective, lasting measure. Education, and the appreciation of nature in our young people, is an enduring method to help protect our environment. If today's children learn to care for their local outside world, and learn of its unique and limited powers, the entire planet will benefit.

The activities in this chapter are designed to aquaint children with the nature of their neighborhood. Learning about light, in color awareness drawing, will take them outside to notice the changes that occur in shadows, tones, and values. The children should learn to associate the color they are seeing with the shining sun. Without the sun, we would have no light, heat, or life as we know it. The study of fire may take place while the children work on charcoal drawings or sand candles. Sand and clay are explored through sand painting, hand building with clay, and clay impressions. The goal of these activities is to have the children begin to associate their lives with the outside world. The closer children feel to the forces of nature, the more understanding they will have of the world around them.

COLOR AWARENESS DRAWING

People often stereotype colors in nature assuming grass is green, clouds are white, and the sky is blue. Color awareness drawing is designed to let children become more aware that colors found in nature are an ever-changing mixture of shades—that the sky is not just blue, but also grey, purple, red, orange, yellow, black, or white. The children will take three walks in one day to an outdoor spot and record the colors seen. Have the children up and ready to notice the colors at sunrise; later, view the hues of an early afternoon; and return again to the spot at twilight, or just as the sun is setting. Explain to the children that the sun, our closest star, is providing all of the light that creates the colors we are seeing.

Outdoor Activity
Time Needed: Three 30-minute periods in one day (sunrise, noon, sunset)
Materials Needed: Box of pastels, a variety of watercolors, paper, brushes, and drawing boards

1. Have the children go to a nearby spot just before sunrise with paper and colors. As they work, have them concentrate on color, rather than be overly concerned with distinctive shapes or lines. Have them choose and mix the colors that seem closest to what they are actually observing. If a tree appears to be made up of dark browns with hints of green, grey, and red, have those colors appear on the paper.

2. Return to the same spot two more times throughout the day. Have the children draw the colors of the same area and notice the changes. Mark on the page what time of the day it was.

3. Make a total of three different drawings, noticing color changes, shadow changes, temperature changes, and compare the differences brought out by these three color studies.

Where Does Light Come From?

1. In our solar system, our sun is the light source. The sun is 93 million miles away from the earth. It takes 8 minutes for the light we see to travel from the sun to earth.

2. Simply put, the sun is a giant thermonuclear reactor burning hydrogen into helium. Light is the waste product put off as the

Figure 4–2 The day's color varies as the sunlight changes.

hydrogen is made into helium. Our sun, believed to be about 10 billion years old, is only in the middle of its life.

3. The moon's light is the reflected light of the sun.

4. The light that humans see is only one part of the spectrum. Different animals see different parts of the spectrum. For example, rattlesnakes have infrared receptors, using heat detection to "see" their world.

5. The different colors we see during the morning, afternoon, and evening are the result of the different angles at which light rays intercept with the atmosphere. For example, when longer wave lengths predominate, at sunset, they act as a filter allowing only some colors to be visible, such as the reds of alpenglow.

6. The reds and brilliant colors we see at sunrise and sunset are also the result of pollution, or particles in the atmosphere. These particles also act as filters.

7. Besides sunlight, other sources of light reside in phosphorescent fireflies, a variety of mushrooms, and bioluminescent fish that glow in the ocean.

CHARCOAL DRAWING

Walking through most forests, a group will often find areas where there are fire scars. Within these burned areas there will be trees with charcoal deposits that can be used as drawing tools. Charcoal is an excellent drawing tool for experimentation. It may crumble readily, so one must be prepared for unexpected change on the drawing paper. Charcoal can be rubbed with the fingers for effective shading results. Charcoal can also be followed by a watercolor brush and a small amount of water to make interesting effects.

Figure 4–3 Charcoal for drawing can be found in fire pits or on burnt trees.

Outdoor Activity

Time Needed: 30 Minutes

Materials Needed: Found charcoal (from burnt trees, near railroad
     tracks, in barbeque pits), drawing paper, watercolor brushes,
     drawing boards

1. Take a walk with the children to an area where you know
   there are available charcoal deposits. Have the children
   look for pieces to draw with.

2. Experiment with the charcoal by drawing lines, shapes,
   and pictures of the trees the charcoal came from. Have
   the children rub the charcoal with their figures to provide
   shading for their drawings.

3. After the drawing is finished have the children experiment using the watercolor brushes and water, a different
   style called a "wash."

What Is Fire Ecology?

1. Each year most of the 100,000 forest fires in the United
States are started by people, either accidentally or by arson. Some
are begun by lightning; but most lightning-caused fires put themselves out, usually after burning less than a quarter-acre of land.

2. One usually thinks of forest fires as a terrible destructive
force. In human terms, it does appear that way. Yet, most natural
forest fires, as opposed to man-made forest fires, can actually be
beneficial to plants and animals in the long run.

3. Fire ecology, or ecopyrology, is the study of how fire affects
the cycles of an environment. For each different terrain, whether it
be forest, sage, chapparal, or an urban area, fire has a different ef-
fect.

4. Many trees actually depend on fire for their reproduction.
Heat from a fire causes the seed coats to open up permanently,
allowing the seeds to be released. Examples of trees and shrubs
that rely on fire are the jack pine, lodgepole pine, giant sequoia,
manzanita, and the ceanothus.

5. Fire burns the debris on the forest floor. By ridding the
ground of the leaves, branches, and dying matter, fire exposes the

soil to sun and moisture, allowing seedlings to germinate and grow.

6. Over the ages, fires were natural parts of the forest community. When natural fires are suppressed by human intervention, the whole forest community is greatly altered. For example, without fire, white fir and Douglas fir gradually replaced the ponderosa pine, which is dependent on the fire's heat.

7. Ceanothus shrubs are a vital food source for elk and deer. If a fire doesn't occur, the Ceanothus won't thrive, and the deer and elk will perhaps starve.

8. Fire is a quick method of decomposition. The blaze releases the nutrients from the plant matter back into the soil very rapidly. A blackened, burnt area will be a source of rich new green growth usually within a few years.

9. With the new fire ecology, there are places today, such as national parks, where fires are actually allowed to burn naturally, unless they are near human habitation. The Park Service is also starting fires of its own to counterbalance the suppression of fires that went on for so many years. These "control burns" are set and maintained to try to restore the forests to their natural state.

GRAB-BAG DRAWINGS

Touch can trigger a child's imagination as much as vision, and children's sense of touch can be encouraged by creating a drawing by touch only. In grab-bag drawings, the groups divide up and gather objects found from nature and place them in paper sacks for the other groups. Rather than looking at an object, the children feel it and then draw the object while it is hidden in the sack. This gives a new dimension to the object. Through the sense of touch, children may become aware of a leaf's fragility, a pine cone's pattern, or a stone's smoothness.

Indoor or Outdoor Activity

Time Needed: ½ hour

Materials Needed: Objects from nature, paper sacks, drawing paper, and drawing tools

Figure 4–4 Grab-bag drawing allows the children to draw nature's textures.

1. Disperse the group to find objects from nature that they can hold in their hands. Collect these objects in a sack.

2. Explain to the children that they will be drawing these objects by feeling them only, without seeing them.

3. With one person holding the sack, several others may reach in at once and feel for a single object and begin to draw it. Allow several minutes to let them draw.

4. If the group is large, use several sacks and have everyone work in groups.

5. After all are finished, empty the sack and see if the child can find the object he or she drew.

6. The child will become aware of objects' shapes and textures through the sense of touch.

What Makes Some Rocks Round and Smooth?

1. Rocks that are round and smooth are often that way because they have been moved and formed by water and ice.

2. Other forms of erosion, such as wind, weather, and human use have worn many stones smooth to the touch.

3. In some places one can find large granite slabs of polished stone. In areas where glaciers advanced, even if it was 50,000 years

ago, there is still evidence of their movement in the form of glacial polish.

4. Boulders are in a continuous process of being broken down by erosion. Rocks that end up in a river or stream bank get transported and rolled along by the current, smoothing and rounding down the rocks, eventually to sand.

5. The rate at which a rock cools from a liquid state to a solid influences its shape and texture. For example, the most rapid cooling of lava results in a black, glasslike rock called obsidian.

6. The smooth five- and six-sided crystals we see are formed as a result of a combination of the elements in their molecular makeup and the temperature at which they cooled and were formed.

7. An important thing to keep in mind is that flat, smooth rocks make excellent skipping stones. This is an ancient and entertaining activity for kids of all ages.

NATURE COLLAGE

The word *collage* is derived from the French verb *coller*, meaning "to glue." To initiate a nature collage, the children go on a collecting walk in their local environment to find different leaves, seed pods, lichens, and sticks. These objects are then arranged on a piece of cardboard. This activity should be done four times a year, each collage reflecting a different season's change or growth. The seasonal collages can be displayed, exhibiting the children's findings over the course of a year.

Indoor or Outdoor Activity
Time Needed: 1 hour/4 times a year
Materials Needed: Found objects from nature, glue, 12-in. by 12-in. square of cardboard, scissors

1. Have the children take a walk and gather objects from nature in a paper sack.

Figure 4–5 Glueing down a nature collage is a process which requires careful handling of plants.

2. Cut the square of cardboard and distribute the glue. Have the children arrange the objects on the collage before being glued down. There are preserving fixatives on the market to spray over the glued collage, so the foliage will retain its colors. Even if you decide not to spray the collage, each season's findings will be different.

3. A border of seeds or beans adds a finished touch to the collage. Arrange the beans around the collage in a repeating pattern and glue them down.

4. Do these collages quarterly and then assemble them all together after one year. Have the children notice the seasonal changes of their findings.

What Are Nature's Adhesives?

1. Barnacles make the strongest known glue. There are 800 species of barnacles. All attach themselves for life with their self-

made cement to pilings, rocks, hulls, and docks. Paleontologists have found fossils of barnacles, similar to today's species, that attached themselves to rocks 150 million years ago.

2. Pine pitch is very sticky. The tree puts out pitch as a scab that forms on any injured part of the tree. Pitch turns into amber, which has a golden-red, glasslike quality; in it are sometimes preserved insects. People have made beautiful jewelry from amber.

3. Many insects make sticky substances to enable their homes to attach to trees or rocks. For example, wasps, bees, and a caterpillar's cocoon employ sticky substances that the insects are able to make themselves.

4. A spider's web uses sticky substances to trap its prey. The frog's tongue is also sticky on the end to help catch its fast-moving prey.

5. The inside of a flower is often sticky. Pollen is taken from flower to flower by insects, birds, bats, the wind, and water, and this sticky substance captures the migrated pollen in the flower to enable potential fertilization.

6. There are mechanical means of adhering objects in nature. Many seeds have evolved with tiny hooks on them. These hooks attach themselves to any traveler who brushes by them, whether that be the fur of a coyote, a bumblebee's back, or the wool socks of a fifth-grader. The seeds then get transported and dropped off somewhere else for germination.

CIRCLE DRAWING

For a spontaneous group activity, a circle drawing is excellent. A circle drawing is created when a group of children creates an on-the-spot story in a drawing. Each person is given one minute to make a contribution on a piece of paper as it goes around the circle. The mystery grows for those who initiated the drawing: How will the story picture end up when it returns to them? The children will be contributing to a group piece, and this often makes a child feel less self-conscious about drawing. Suggest at the start that the picture story take place in an outdoor setting that is familiar to them. The picture can include weather, wildlife, and personal adventure.

Indoor or Outdoor Activity
Time Needed: 30 minutes
Materials Needed: Drawing papers, pencils, drawing boards

1. With the group seated in a circle, discuss the purpose of circle drawing. Mention that they will each be contributing to a story as the paper comes to them. Explain that the story should take place outdoors and can include familiar sights, people, weather changes, and animals.

2. Pass out the drawing tools.

3. Let the children know they each have one minute to add their contribution. They then will pass the drawing to the next person.

4. Continue until the drawing goes around the entire circle.

5. After completion, have the first child and the last each interpret what they think the circle drawing is about.

Ask the group if any one can tell what they think the drawing is about

What Are Some Cycles in Nature?

1. Cycles are like circles, they have no beginning and no end. Cycles in nature are always in the process, no matter how slow, of becoming something else.

2. Water goes in a cycle. It has three forms in this cycle: a solid—ice, snow; liquid—water; gas—vapor, steam. Start with the most familiar form of water, its liquid form, in a backyard birdbath. The sun shines down on the birdbath causing the water to heat up and change to a gas in the process of evaporation. This vapor rises into the atmosphere to form clouds. When the clouds get cold, the vapor freezes and forms snow. The snow falls down into the backyard birdbath. The sun comes out and melts the snow to a liquid. The cycle is complete. The water cycle depends upon the sun or some other source of heat.

3. Life goes in a cycle. Plants and animals begin life as tiny seeds. They are nurtured and fed and grow into young plants and animals. They begin to mature and develop methods to reproduce themselves. They are fertilized when the male and female are joined together. Through fertilization, the new seed begins a life

Earth Science

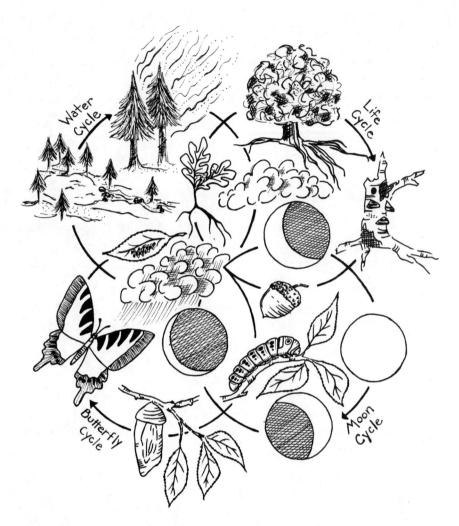

Figure 4–6 This diagram illustrates four examples of the cycles in nature.

and the now old plant and animal dies and returns to the soil, enabling new growth to occur.

SCULPTURES FROM NATURE

Sculptures made from sand, mud, or snow are art forms that can blow apart or melt away hours after the children complete their work. But the transitory quality of these materials does not dim the children's imaginations. The following activity is explained using snow as the medium, but can also be done in mud or sand.

Outdoor Activity
Time Needed: 30 minutes
Materials Needed: Snow and mittens

1. Talk with the children about how different animals survive in the winter. Their various adaptations for survival include camouflage, wide feet, claws, wings, fur, feathers, hibernation, and migration.

2. Let the children divide into teams of three, and have them sculpt an animal from their imagination. Their goal should be to design an animal that is perfectly adapted for the immediate environment. They can use a variety of characteristics obtained from their knowledge of how animals survive. For example, they may sculpt a creature with a hard turtle shell, that has wings, and a long trunk to dig beneath the snow for food.

3. Have the children introduce their snow sculpture to the rest of the group. They should be prepared to explain its name, its methods of survival, its predators, and its food sources.

Where Does Snow Come From?

1. For snow to form, a cloud must be chilled to a few degrees above or below 0°C. The cloud droplets are supercooled and freeze together into crystals. Because the crystals carry a thin film of unfrozen water, they mat into snowflakes when they collide.

2. In extreme cold the crystals are drier and fall as granular snow. Rain that starts in warm air and falls through a cold layer turns, not into snow, but into ice pellets called *sleet*.

3. Hailstones originate as frozen raindrops in high clouds, which move through thunderstorms and are hurled about in updrafts, picking up layers of snow and ice.

4. Mountains are a storehouse for falling snow, slowly releasing it down into the lowlands through streams as the spring thaw begins. Sometimes these spring thaws bring floods, depending on how deep a snowfall the winter provided and how warm the spring is.

*Earth
Science*

117

Figure 4–7 A two-person snow shelter provides a fun winter dwelling.

5. Snow is an excellent insulator. Many small animals escape freezing winds and subzero temperatures by burrowing under the snow. These animals are called *subnivian*—those which live beneath the snow.

6. The insulation factor of snow also keeps the soil from freezing. If the ground froze, many hibernating species—insects, worms, chipmunks—would die of cold.

7. Snow allows fungi and bacteria to remain active, sometimes all winter, decomposing litter on the ground floor.

FLOATING OBJECTS FROM NATURE

Pieces of bark and branches, seed pods, and shells all turn into floating vessels when launched on a body of water. The river's current can be visibly demonstrated when children race their boats downstream. Sails can be constructed out of leaves and small fabric scraps with sticks and glue. Children will create many stories and games around water when allowed to wade and float their boats.

Outdoor Activity

Time Needed: 15 minutes

Materials Needed: A water body (fountain, stream, pond, pool), objects from nature (bark, sticks, leaves, walnut shells), toothpicks and fabric scraps, glue and pocket knives

1. Have the children collect the sticks, pieces of bark, shells, and other materials needed to construct their boats. The piece of bark should be flat, perhaps 3-in. by 5-in. With the pocket knife, cut a hole in the middle of the "boat." Put a large leaf through a stick, and place the stick as a mast in the hole of the boat. Or use fabric scraps. A sense of balance and centering on the boat is needed when adding a sail.

2. A stream's shape and speed are affected by currents, eddies, and seasonal runoff. Discuss this with the group. They will better understand how their boats travel.

What Are Eddies and Currents?

1. *Currents* are a mass of water flowing in a definite direction because of gravity. The speed of water's flow, or its current, is an important factor in its erosive powers. A steep, fast-moving stream pushes not only water but fine particles, mineral salts, pebbles, gravel, and even boulders downhill.

2. As the river slows down the larger stones are left behind. And soon the smaller stones are deposited as the stream sorts its load by its speed.

3. Rivers tend to follow the shortest and easiest course heading downhill. This cut is usually a V-shaped carving process.

4. *Eddies* are fluid currents that move against the general flow. Similar to whirlpools, eddies are formed oftentimes when they flow around an obstacle. A flow that is composed largely of eddies is called *turbulent*.

Figure 4–8 The children discover the creek's current while launching twigs and leaf boats.

5. Turbidity occurs in the ocean when there are dense, flowing masses of sediment-carrying water at speeds of 50 miles per hour. These are often begun by earthquake disturbances on the continental shelves and slopes.

6. High water inevitably occurs in the spring when the winter snows melt, running down the mountains to the low country.

7. Few streams follow straight courses. On floodplains they tend to flow in looping curves known as *meanders*. The pattern of these curves is continuously changing. They change as the slow-moving water on the inside of the bend drops its load of sediments and builds sandbars. Faster-moving currents on the outside of the bend cut under the bank and gradually extend the curve.

SAND CANDLES

Earth
Science

Candles today are more popular than ever. With sand candles, children can create a candle of any shape or design. A bucket of sand is needed to form the negative shape that the paraffin is poured into. *Paraffin* is a distillate of wood, coal, or petroleum; developed in the nineteenth century, it soon became the main form of candle wax. Before paraffin, beeswax and tallow were used ever since Roman times. Shapes for molding can be made with a bowl or cylinder—and then removed to pour the paraffin into the sand—or more original shapes can be created by merely digging a form in the sand with the hands.

Indoor or Outdoor Activity
Time Needed: 2 hours, work time
Materials Needed: Cotton string, 1 tb. salt, 1 tb. borax, 1 box paraffin, sand, access to stove, double boiler pans, candy thermometer

Figure 4–9 Sand candles are molded by the children's hands before the melted paraffin is poured.

1. The children make the wicks by using a strong cotton string, which needs to soak overnight in 1 tb. salt and 1 tb. of borax dissolved in 1 cup of water. Hang the string up to dry and stiffen it by dipping it in melted paraffin.

2. Essowax and Gulfwax are the two most common commercial brands of paraffin. To melt the paraffin, set up a double boiler with 3 inches of water in the bottom pan and 1 block of paraffin in the top pan. Use a thermometer and check the temperature often. The paraffin is combustible at 290°F, but should not get hotter than 215°F because it smokes and turns brown.

3. The sand should be slightly damp to hold the melted paraffin. Have the children mold a shape with a bowl or with their hands. Their first shape should be about the size of a grapefruit.

4. Put the wick in the center of the shape and keep the wick's upper end taut while pouring the paraffin into the shape. The temperature of the paraffin should be about 200°F for pouring. It will take 1 hour to harden and 6 hours to completely cool.

5. After removing the hardened candle from the sand, it is best to either dip it in 180°F paraffin for 2 seconds, or dip it into boiling water, holding it by the wick, for 3 to 4 seconds. Follow this by dipping it into cold water for a few seconds. This will keep the outside sand from shedding.

Where Did Fire Come From?

1. The original and only source of fire for a very long time was lightning. The earliest unquestionable fire users were the Peking humans, who lived about 500,000 B.C.

2. It was not until 7000 B.C. that people developed reliable fire-making tools in the form of drills, saws, and other friction-producing implements. Flint was used to strike a spark against pyrites. At this time, it was still easier to keep a fire alive than to have to reignite it.

3. Fire became one of humankind's essential tools to control the environment and start the development of civilization. The

earliest uses of fire were heating, cooking, and burning under-brush to hunt and kill animals.

4. When people burned back the underbrush, grasslands be-gan to develop, encouraging more animals to graze. These grass-lands became great hunting grounds.

5. People discovered that the leftover ash from fires is a valua-ble fertilizer.

6. For centuries fire was used in religious rituals. Many leg-ends and myths gave fire an origin, from the Native American's ver-sion of Coyote stealing fire to the Greek myth of Prometheus steal-ing fire from the gods.

7. The first industrial use of fire was in firing pottery in un-derground kilns.

8. From the Neolithic period on, the uses of fire have carried through all time.

PREPARING NATURAL CLAY

Pottery is an ancient art, dating back 7000 years. The earliest pot-ters formed their clay next to river banks and swamps. In ancient Crete, Egypt, Greece, China, and South America succeeding gener-ations of potters contributed techniques and styles, leaving dis-tinctive marks on their pottery. Today's potters can still use a simi-lar method to draw clay out of the ground, as did the potters of long ago. The following activity describes how one can prepare natural clay.

Outdoor Activity
Time Needed: A couple of days
Materials Needed: A natural clay bed, newspapers, ¼-in. mesh
   sieve, coffee cans, hammer or pounding rocks, water, window
   screen wire, cloth bowls, shovels

1. Inquire around the local area as to where a clay deposit would be available to you. For information, contact a local college's botany or art department, a Forest Service office, a local farmer or rancher, or a nearby ceramics shop. These people know the clay conditions in their area.

2. Select a clay deposit that is as free as possible from impurities—that is, sand, gravel, dirt, plant roots, and so forth. Dig enough clay to fill the coffee cans.

3. Spread the clay out on the newspaper and place it in the sun to dry completely.

4. The clay will dry in hard lumps. With the hammer or rocks, break up the lumps to a fine powder. Do not crush any rock into the clay; be sure to remove the rocks.

5. Sift the powder clay through the sieve and remove the pebbles.

6. Fill the can with the sifted clay two-thirds full. Cover the clay with water until it is completely saturated and covered to the top of the can.

7. Using hands, stir the clay to evenly distribute the water throughout.

8. Soak this for two hours or until the mixture is the consistency of thick cream.

9. Pour this cream mixture through a piece of window screen into another can.

10. Let this strained mixture sit overnight, or until the clay has settled to the bottom. Pour off the clear liquid on top. Try not to stir up the thick "slip" underneath.

11. Pour the remaining thick slip into the cloth-lined bowls. As the cloth absorbs the water, the slip stiffens and separates from the cloth. The clay is then ready to store in covered cans. Clay improves with age. It should be stored wetter than needed to work with, because the clay will dry out when taken out of cans to be used and wedged.

12. Wedge the clay before using it. Wedging is the thorough pounding and repeated slicing of the clay to get rid of air bubbles inside it.

Where Does Clay Come From?

1. Clay comes from tiny soil particles less than 0.005 millimeters large. Along with the clay minerals, most clays also include decayed organic materials and quartz. Clay rock includes clay shales, mudstones, sedimentary rock, marine sediments, glacial clays, deep-sea clays, and ceramic clays.

2. Clay is moldable when wet, yet sticks together and remains coherent when dry. It is an earth material that has great uses and importance worldwide.

3. The clay within soil provides the environment for almost all plant growth. Clay provides the necessary processes that soils must have to support plant life, such as water retention, porousness, and the ability to expose soil to the air and absorb it.

4. The use of clay in pottery has allowed anthropologists to record human history. Such clay vessels have been tools of function and beauty for centuries.

5. Clay has been used as a brick-building and tile-making material since very early times.

6. White clay, or *kaolin*, has been used as paper coating and filler. It also allows the paper to be printable and gives it a gloss.

7. Clays have been used in making rubber. They increase the rubber's resistance to wear and help eliminate mold from developing.

CLAY IMPRESSIONS

Fossils are formed in the earth's crust by organisms impacted in the shifting layers over a period of time. Children can create their own fossil impressions with clay and objects from nature. By pressing leaves, fish skeletons, or shells into clay, an impression of the object is made. This imprinted image in clay will dry and harden, and retain the detail of the minute patterns found in nature. The children can arrange a variety of objects and make an imprint of multiple images.

Indoor or Outdoor Activity
Time Needed: 30 minutes
Materials Needed: Clay, newspaper, cardboard, objects from nature (leaves, shells, fish skeletons, dead insects), tweezers

1. Prepare a slab of clay by flattening a fist-size ball of clay and rolling it smooth and ½-in. thick.

Earth
Science

125

2. Gather together a variety of leaves, ferns, insects, shells, or any other found object that can be imprinted into the clay.

3. Lay one or more of the objects on the slab and press them gently under a stiff piece of cardboard.

4. Carefully lift off the cardboard. With the tweezers, carefully pull out the nature objects from the clay, and discover the print that has formed. Experiment with different shapes and arrangements.

5. One use for these imprinted images is to cut them up into individual pieces. Drill a small hole at the top of each impression. Tie strings through the holes and make a mobile out of the dried clay pieces.

Where Do Fossils Come From?

1. The fossil record is the key to the earth's history. Fossils are the remains and traces of plants and animals that are preserved in the earth's crust.

2. There are two situations in which an organism might become fossilized. The first is by being buried very rapidly which would slow down decomposition and inhibit scavengers. In the second, the organism might possess hard parts capable of being fossilized. Freezing may also preserve organisms.

3. The hard shells of clams and snails are commonly found in sedimentary rocks. Fossilized shells and bones have often been slightly altered as their parts are made more dense by added mineral matter, such as calcium and iron that adheres to the fossilizing materials.

4. The study of fossil plants is called *paleobotany*. Fossilized algae has been discovered in rocks that are 2 billion years old. The plants that are most frequently seen fossilized are twigs, leaves, and fruits found in shale, siltstone, and limestone. Petrified wood is a type of preserved fossil rock.

5. The earliest known fossil vertebrates occur in rocks around 500 million years old. The remains of these marine animals are made up of pieces of the bony armor that covered their bodies. Through studying fossils, scientists know how successful and di-

verse the vertebrates have been. Fossilized animals with some sort of backbone have been found equipped to survive the sea, land, and air.

HANDBUILDING WITH CLAY

Since ancient times potters have been handbuilding with clay. Classic earthenware forms evolved based on utility and convenience, but also on what was pleasing to the eye. There are several classic styles when making pots by hand, such as coil pots, thumb-press pots, and slab pots. Children will be more experimental in their pottery designs when shown a variety of clay forms.

Indoor or Outdoor Activity
Time Needed: 1 hour to build a pot and several days to dry it
Materials Needed: Clay, water bowls, flat working surface, cutting tools

1. Take a mound of clay and knead it, like kneading bread. Pound the clay repeatedly down on the table to make it

Figure 4–10 The boy is rolling out a slab to make clay impressions.

supple and take out the air bubbles. This is called "wedging" the clay.

2. After the clay is wedged, cut it into mounds that the children can handle easily.

3. Explain they are to make a pot using one of the three methods described. Mention that their pot's walls should be an equal width and that the bottom should be the same thickness as the walls.

4. Coil Method: Make several long thin coils by rolling the clay with the hands. All of the coils should be about the same length. They should be kept under a damp cloth. The base should be cut from a slab or built from coils. As the coils are carefully wound around the base, one on top

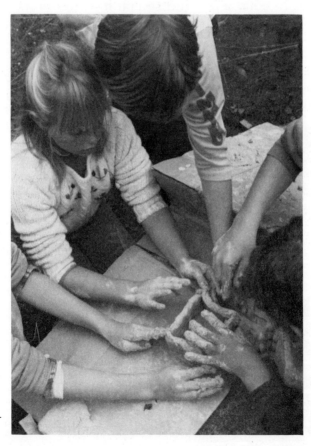

Figure 4–11 A slab pot comes together with the aid of many hands.

of another, adhere them with very wet clay. This wet clay adhesive is referred to as "slip."

5. Thumb-press Method: Start with an oval shape. Have the children press their thumbs in the center of the oval and smooth the outside and the inside with slip.

6. Slab Method: Roll out ¼-in. wide slabs that are about 6 to 10 in. long. Cut them out using a pointed-edge tool, such as a pointed stick or scissors. Cut a rectangular slab. Roll this rectangle into a cylinder shape. Seal the seam with slip. Stand the cylinder on another slab and cut around the end of the cylinder to form the bottom. Seal these seams with slip.

What Is Adobe?

1. *Adobe* structures are those made from clay soil bricks; it is the Spanish word for sun-dried bricks.

2. Adobe bricks date back thousands of years in several parts of the world. This is a popular method of construction in places where the climate is dry or semidry, such as North Africa, Spain, the Southwest United States, and Peru.

3. People have made adobe the same way for ages. The process begins by wetting a clay soil and allowing it to stand for a few days to soften, and then by breaking up the clods. The next step is to add a quantity of straw or some type of local fibrous material. This mixture is combined with a hoe, and the final trampling is done with bare feet. At the proper consistency, the adobe is molded into brick shapes. These bricks are allowed to dry in the sun, flat on the ground, and then are stacked on edge to permit a final drying. The Indians built their walls with these adobe bricks, allowing each layer to dry before adding the next wet layer.

4. The advantages of using adobe for construction are its availability, its cheapness, and its ability to insulate.

MOBILES FROM NATURE

Gathering "found objects" from outside and arranging them in a balanced, hanging sculpture creates a mobile from nature.

Figure 4–12 A Boy Scouts leader decorates his yard with the mobile his troop made for him.

Alexander Calder, one of the first artists to make mobiles a popular art form, was inspired by nature's organic forms in constructing his art. Often, a theme is used in the selecting of objects from the local environment, for example, sea shells, walnut shells, mosses, or driftwood. One should collect more objects than one plans to use so that one can be selective when choosing the items. Items that work best for balance in shape, color, and weight should be chosen. Using simple objects as a beautiful tribute to the world around us, these mobiles will hang gracefully within the natural environment.

Outdoor Activity

Time Needed: 1 hour

Materials Needed: Cotton thread, scissors, "found objects" from nature

1. Walk outside and stop in a quiet place. Have the children look around and gather materials with which they will construct their mobile.

2. Have them tie the objects to the sticks, allowing several inches of thread to hang between the object and the stick. The children should hold the stick in the middle while hanging the objects, to give a sense of balance to the construction.

3. After they are finished, rather than carry them home, have the children find a special private "spot" away from the group and the trail, where they can hang their mobile.

4. Perhaps another adventurer will come upon the mobiles, but even if it is not for a long time, each mobile-maker will have a clear image of where his or her mobile is hanging as part of the forest.

Where Does the Wind Come From?

1. Wind is the result of the upper atmosphere attempting to equalize pressure. The different pressures result from the earth's rotation and the sun. We do not feel these winds directly, but they are the drivers of storm systems.

2. The winds we feel occur closer to the earth's surface. Offshore and onshore breezes are easy to understand. Offshore breezes occur when heat rises over the ocean at night, creating a vacuum that is filled by blowing winds that flow into the space. Onshore breezes occur when the heat rises off the land during the day; the breeze returns onto the shore to fill in that void.

3. Just as there are different currents in a water system, the air moves as a fluid. There may be several different weather patterns occurring at the same time in different levels of the atmosphere. The air flows with one pattern in a higher atmosphere and a different one closer to the earth's surface.

4. Wind power is becoming popular again as a method to generate energy. On the back of a monthly utility bill there will probably be a toll-free energy conservation number that you can

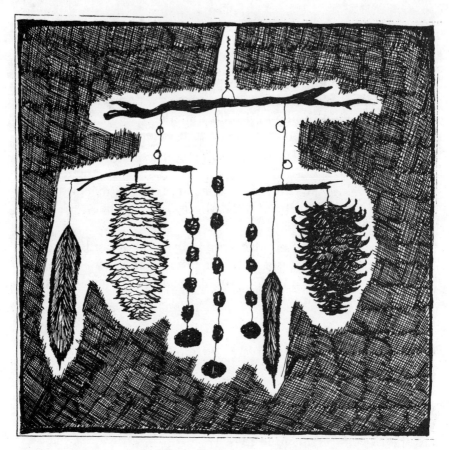

Figure 4–13 The wind helps to display the balanced hanging mobile.

call to find out how much wind power is being used in your local area.

5. Wind is a great carrier of seeds, pollen, and animal life. Spiders have traveled all the way to Hawaii via their traveling webs, called gossamers, caught in high trade winds.

SAND PAINTING

Sand can be collected and used as paint, especially if it is collected at different locations such as a lakeshore, the desert, the ocean, or along a river. Children will see that sand granules contain a variety of colors and textures. Storing the collected sand in clear glass jars, labeled where each was gathered, will make this color variation more apparent to the children. Once four or more jars of sand have been collected, the children can begin to paint a design with sand.

Indoor or Outdoor Activity
Time Needed: 1 hour
Materials Needed: At least four different colors of sand; glue, cardboard, markers, newspaper

1. Before starting, discuss with the group where the jars of sand came from and why the sand is made up of different colors, and then explain how the sand will be used in the project.
2. Have the children draw a design on their cardboard with the dark-colored marker.

Figure 4–14 Pouring and drawing with sand is a timeless art which the Indians of the Southwest have kept alive.

Earth Science

3. Each child should work with one color of sand at a time. Have them spread glue evenly in one section of their design, then, over a newspaper, have them pour one color of sand over that glued section. Press gently on the poured sand with the fingers. Any excess sand should be shaken off onto the newspaper and then poured back into the proper jar. Continue with the glue and another color of sand, until the whole design has been covered.

4. If a variety of sand colors are hard to find, or the colors are not as bright as you would like them, you can dye the sand different colors. Fill the glass jar two-thirds full of sand. Drip in the food dye of the desired color. Close the jar and shake it until most of the sand is the desired color. Spread the sand out on a newspaper until it is completely dry. Pour it back into the jars until you are ready to use it.

Why Are Sands Different Colors?

1. *Sand* is defined as being loose, granular particles of worn or broken-down rock, finer than gravel and coarser than dust. Sand is eroded rock. It has so many colors because there are many different colored rocks. There are three main divisions in rocks.

   a. *Igneous* rocks were once molten and come from deep inside the earth. They have cooled at different speeds and assume a variety of colors ranging from white, pink, and green to shiny black.

   b. *Sedimentary* rocks are formed by layers of sand and clay that are washed down into lake beds and ocean floors. They become cemented under pressure and often are raised up again by later earth movements. Sandstone breaks down easily into colored sand particles such as reds, browns, and yellows.

   c. *Metamorphic* rock is formed when rock is changed in form through heat and pressure during periods of deep burial. Slate was once clay, quartzite came from sandstone, and marble is metamorphosed limestone. Again, with these different types of rock come a variety of colors.

2. These three types of rock undergo erosion through the powers of wind, ice, streams, gravity, and people. Friction breaks

the rock into sand, which then is easily transported to collecting places along the shores of oceans, rivers, and creeks—and left in huge deposits found in deserts.

3. Sand is chiefly composed of the igneous materials quartz, feldspar, and bits of mica. The mountain's granite becomes eroded, and rain washes this sand down into the lowlands.

4. Some beach sands, called *basalt* rock, were produced by volcanic ash, originally black lava; other sands come from broken shells and coral materials. White sand often comes from broken-down coral rock, and pink sand can come from sea shells.

BOX RELIEF

Miniature worlds have always fascinated young and old alike. From collections of priceless antique miniature figurines, to dime-store snow scenes captured in a glass-dome shaker, people love to admire and construct miniatures. Perhaps this is because minia-

Figure 4–15 A box relief done by a group requires discussion and cooperation.

tures allow us to put the immense size of the earth in perspective, much as our perspective is changed when a land area is viewed from an airplane for the first time. Environments take on a more limited framework, rivers have origins and eventual places they flow into, deserts no longer appear endless, and the mountains fit into the landscape without dominating it. Children can construct a relief environment called a box relief based on a place they have visited. This activity will help them remember the landscape and its natural resources, as well as serve as a memento of their visit.

Indoor or Outdoor Activity
Time Needed: 1 hour
Materials Needed: Cardboard boxes; objects from nature such as rocks, sand, leaves, sticks; paper, pencil, colors, and scissors

1. After returning from an outing, draw a map on paper of the place visited. Discuss with the children the geographical features of the area visited.

2. Have the children make constructions in their boxes. Cut the sides of the boxes down low enough so the children can easily reach into them. Have them recreate water bodies, mountains, and buildings. Have them use the rocks, sand, leaves, ferns, and colors to replicate the features of the landscape.

3. The children will remember their visited area longer by making this construction, and it will help them put into perspective the limitations of one area in comparison to the great size of the globe. Putting things in miniature will give the children a perspective on how infinitesimal we are in comparison to the earth, and how small the earth is in comparison to the universe.

How Does the Earth's Surface Change Forms?

1. Weathering and erosion are the processes that explain how rocks are worn away and soil is removed and deposited elsewhere. *Diastrophism* is the term used to explain the process by which the earth's crust is upturned, broken, slanted, and folded.

These three forces explain the ever-changing face of the earth's surface. Most of the forces of diastrophism are deep within the earth, hidden in the earth's plates and molten rock, while erosion works openly upon the surface.

2. The greatest force of erosion is moving water. An estimated 10 million billion gallons of water runs off to the seas every year, pulling with it millions of tons of mud, clay, and mineral fragments. These moving minerals change the face of the earth, carving valleys, changing a river's course, and depositing sandbars.

3. The ocean does not erode the earth as much as swift streams, but along some vulnerable coastlines the ocean's waves crash onto the shore with a force of 3 tons to the square foot. The ocean can build up as well as break down. Where the shore is gently sloping with a shallow bottom, the waves deposit the sand on shore-forming sandbars. These sandbars may grow enough to enclose a lagoon, creating a new habitat for living things.

4. The core of the earth is believed to be between 4000°F and 8000°F. Here on the surface we are hardly aware of the furnace below us. Through the changing forces of geysers, hot springs, and especially volcanoes, we are made conscious of the heat deep within the earth. Volcanic eruptions spread their outpourings of lava, gases, and ash onto the surface, creating a different land form.

5. Earthquakes and their fault lines change the contours of the earth's surface by their sudden movements. The aftermath of an earthquake often includes landslides, fires, and tidal waves that further reshape the surfaces of the earth.

6. Our solid earth is not as solid as it appears. The rocks are undergoing a constant change, just as all things are, but usually these shifts are on a very slow and large scale.

Bibliography

The more time I spend outside, the more I realize how much there is to learn about nature. It is an inexhaustible subject, one that can be explored from the termite's habitat to the constellations of the heavens. The best way to become more familiar with this world is to get outside and walk in it, draw it, and explore its ever-changing face, wet and dry, high and low. John Muir said that "books are but piles of stones set up to show coming travelers where other minds have been." The following bibliography is provided to illustrate supplementary reading material for each of *Nature with Art*'s chapters. Reading "piles of stones" can prepare you for the outings that you as a parent, teacher, or nature guide are interested in sharing with your children.

CHAPTER ONE: PLANT INVESTIGATIONS

ANDREWS, W. A. *A Guide to the Study of Soil Ecology.* Englewood Cliffs, N.J.: Prentice-Hall, Inc., 1973.

HARLOW, WILLIAM M. *Inside Wood, Masterpiece of Nature.* Washington, D.C.: American Forestry Association, 1970.

JACKSON, JAMES P. *The Pulse of the Forest.* Washington, D.C.: American Forestry Association, 1980.

MCCORMICK, JACK. *The Life of the Forest.* New York: McGraw-Hill, Inc., 1966.

ROTH, CHARLES E. *The Plant Observer's Guidebook.* Englewood Cliffs, N.J.: Prentice-Hall, Inc., 1984.

STERN, KINGSLEY. *Introductory Plant Biology.* Dubuque, Iowa: William C. Brown Company Publishers, 1982.

TOMKINS, PETER, AND CHRISTOPHER BIRD. *The Secret Life of Plants.* New York: Harper & Row, 1973.

CHAPTER TWO: ANIMAL EXPLORATIONS

CARRIGHAR, SALLY. *One Day on Beetle Rock. Philadelphia:* Curtis Publishing Company, 1943.

DILLARD, ANNIE. *Pilgrim at Tinker Creek.* New York: Bantam Books, 1974.

GRATER, RUSSELL K. *Discovering Sierra Mammals.* Yosemite, Calif.: Yosemite Natural History Association and Sequoia Natural History Association, 1978.

KLOTS, ALEXANDER B. AND ELSIE. *1001 Questions Answered About Insects.* New York: Dover Publications, Inc., 1961.

LEOPOLD, ALDO. *Sand County Almanac.* New York: Oxford University Press, 1966.

ROMER, ALFRED SHERWOOD. *Man and the Vertebrates.* Chicago, Ill.: University of Chicago Press, 1941.

STORER, TRACY I. AND USINGER, ROBERT L. *General Zoology.* New York: McGraw-Hill Publishers, 1979.

WELTY, JOEL CARL. *The Life of Birds.* New York: Alfred A. Knopf, 1962.

CHAPTER THREE: PEOPLE AND PLACES

BARRETT, SAMUEL ALFRED, AND E. W. GIFFORD. *Miwok Material Culture.* Yosemite, Calif.: Yosemite Natural History Association, 1933.

CLARKE, JAMES MITCHELL. *The Life and Adventures of John Muir.* San Diego, Calif.: The Word Shop Publisher, 1979.

KROEBER, THEODORA. *The Inland Whale.* Berkeley, Calif: University of California Press, 1959.

LA PENA, FRANK, AND CRAIG BATES. *Legends of the Yosemite Miwok.* Yosemite, Calif: Yosemite Natural History Association, 1981.

MINOR, MARZ NONO. *American Indian Craft Book.* New York: Popular Library Edition, 1972.

MUIR, JOHN. *The Wilderness World of John Muir.* Boston: Houghton Mifflin Publishers, 1954.

STORM, HYEMEYOHSTS. *Seven Arrows.* New York: Ballantine Books, Inc., 1973.

THOREAU, HENRY DAVID. *Walden and "Civil Disobedience."* New York: The New American Library of World Literature, 1960.

CHAPTER FOUR: EARTH SCIENCE

BEISER, ARTHUR. *The Earth.* New York: Time-Life Books, 1969.

DE BELL, GARRETT. *The New Environmental Handbook.* San Francisco, Calif.: Friends of the Earth Publishers, 1980.

MCKEARIN, GEORGE AND HELEN. *American Glass.* New York: Crown Publishers, 1948.

NILSSON, LENNART. *Close to Nature.* New York: Pantheon Books, 1984.

OLSON, SIGURD F. *Sigurd F. Olson's Wilderness Days.* New York: Alfred A. Knopf, 1973.

PRINGLE, LAURENCE. *Natural Fire, Its Ecology in Forests.* New York: William Morrow and Company, 1979.

ROSS, MICHAEL. *Cycles, Cycles, Cycles.* Yosemite, Calif.: Yosemite Natural History Association, 1979.

WALLACE, DAVID RAINS. *The Dark Range—A Naturalists Night Notebook.* San Francisco, Calif.: Sierra Club Books, 1978.

RECOMMENDED READING

ARNOLD, ARNOLD. *The Crowell Book of Arts and Crafts for Children.* New York: T. Y. Crowell Publishers, 1975.

CARSON, RACHEL L. *The Sense of Wonder.* New York: Harper & Row Publishers, 1956.

CORNELL, JOSEPH BHARAT. *Sharing Nature with Children.* Grass Valley, Calif.: Ananda Publications, 1979.

FRANCK, FREDERICK. *The Zen of Seeing: Seeing/Drawing as Meditation.* New York: Vintage Books, Random House, 1973.

JANSON, H. W. *History of Art.* Englewood Cliffs, N.J.: Prentice-Hall, Inc., 1977.

KOHL, JUDITH AND HERBERT. *The View from the Oak.* San Francisco, Calif.: Sierra Club Books, 1977.

LABOR, EARLE. *Great Works of Jack London.* New York: Harper & Row Publishers, 1970.

LATHEM, EDWARD CONNERY, ed., *The Poetry of Robert Frost.* New York: Holt, Rinehart and Winston, 1979.

LESLIE, CLARE WALKER. *Nature Drawing: A Tool for Learning.* Englewood Cliffs, N.J.: Prentice-Hall, Inc., 1980.

NICOLAIDES, KIMON. *The Natural Way to Draw.* Boston: Houghton Mifflin Company, 1941.

PREBLE, DUANE. *We Create Art Creates Us.* New York: Harper & Row, 1976.

RUESS, EVERETT. *A Vagabond for Beauty.* Layton, Utah: Peregrine Smith Books, 1983.

RUSSELL, TERRY AND RENNY. *On the Loose.* San Francisco, Calif.: Sierra Club Books and Ballantine Books, 1967.

SERVICE, ROBERT. *Best of Robert Service.* New York: Dodd, Mead and Company, 1953.

SNYDER, GARY. *Turtle Island.* New York: New Directions Books, 1974.

UNTERMEYER, LOUIS. *Robert Frost's Poems.* Pocket Books, 1971.

Index

Index

146